Microsoft®

MCSE

Exam 70-229

AF725449

Microsoft® SQL Server™ 2000 Database Design and Implementation

Readiness Review

Sharon Bjeletich and
Eddy Hahn

PUBLISHED BY
Microsoft Press
A Division of Microsoft Corporation
One Microsoft Way
Redmond, Washington 98052-6399

Library of Congress Cataloging-in-Publication Data
Bjeletich, Sharon.
MCSE Microsoft SQL Server 2000 Database Design and Implementation Readiness Review, Exam 70-229 / Sharon Bjeletich, Eddy Hahn.
p. cm.
Includes index.
ISBN 0-7356-1251-X
1. Electronic data processing personnel--Certification. 2. Microsoft software--Examinations--Study guides. 3. Databases--Design--Examinations. 4. SQL server. I. Hahn, Eddy, 1972- II. Title.

QA76.3 .B547 2001
005.75'85--dc21

2001018331

Printed and bound in the United States of America.

1 2 3 4 5 6 7 8 9 QWE 6 5 4 3 2 1

Distributed in Canada by Penguin Books Canada Limited.

A CIP catalogue record for this book is available from the British Library.

Microsoft Press books are available through booksellers and distributors worldwide. For further information about international editions, contact your local Microsoft Corporation office or contact Microsoft Press International directly at fax (425) 936-7329. Visit our Web site at mspress.microsoft.com. Send comments to *mspinput@microsoft.com*.

Acquisitions Editor: Thomas Pohlmann
Project Editor: Karen Szall
Technical Editor: Jack Beaudry
Manuscript Editor: Margaret Berson

Part No. X08-04914

Contents

Welcome to Microsoft SQL Server 2000 Database Design and Implementation

Welcome to *MCSE Microsoft SQL Server 2000 Database Design and Implementation Readiness Review: Exam 70-229*. The Readiness Review series gives you a focused, timesaving way to identify the information you need to know to pass the Microsoft Certified Professional (MCP) exams. The series combines a realistic electronic assessment with a review book to help you become familiar with the types of questions that you will encounter on the MCP exam. By reviewing the objectives and sample questions, you can focus on the specific skills that you need to improve before taking the exam.

This book helps you evaluate your readiness for the MCP Exam 70-229: Designing and Implementing Databases with Microsoft SQL Server 2000 Enterprise Edition. When you pass this exam, you earn core credit toward Microsoft Certified Systems Engineer (MCSE) certification. In addition, when you pass this exam you achieve Microsoft Certified Professional status.

Note You can find a complete list of MCP exams and their related objectives on the Microsoft Certified Professional Web site at *http://www.microsoft.com/mcp.*

The Readiness Review series lets you identify any areas in which you might need additional training. To help you get the training you need to successfully pass the certification exams, Microsoft Press publishes a complete line of self-paced training kits and other study materials. For comprehensive information about the topics covered in the Designing and Implementing Databases with Microsoft SQL Server 2000 Enterprise Edition exam, see the corresponding MCSE training kit—*Microsoft SQL Server 2000 System Administration*.

Before You Begin

This MCSE Readiness Review consists of two main parts: the Readiness Review electronic assessment program on the accompanying compact disc, and this Readiness Review book.

The Readiness Review Components

The electronic assessment is a practice certification test that helps you evaluate your skills. It provides instant scoring feedback, so you can determine areas in which additional study might be helpful before you take the certification exam. Although your score on the electronic assessment does not necessarily indicate what your score will be on the certification exam, it does give you the opportunity to answer questions that are similar to those on the actual certification exam.

The Readiness Review book is organized by the exam's objectives. Each chapter of the book pertains to one of the six primary groups of objectives on the actual exam, called the Objective Domains. Each Objective Domain lists the tested skills you need to master to adequately answer the exam questions. Because the certification exams focus on real-world skills, the Tested Skills and Suggested Practices lists provide practices that emphasize the practical application of the exam objectives. Each Objective Domain also provides suggestions for further reading or additional resources to help you understand the objectives and increase your ability to perform the task or skills specified by the objectives.

Within each Objective Domain, you will find the related objectives that are covered on the exam. Each objective provides you with the following:

- **Key terms** you must know to understand the objective. Knowing these terms can help you answer the objective's questions correctly.
- Several sample exam questions with the correct answers. The answers are accompanied by explanations of each correct and incorrect answer. (These questions match the questions on the electronic assessment.)

You use the electronic assessment to determine the exam objectives that you need to study, and then use the Readiness Review book to learn more about those particular objectives and discover additional study materials to supplement your knowledge. You can also use the Readiness Review book to research the answers to specific sample test questions. Keep in mind that to pass the exam, you should understand not only the answer to the question, but also the concepts on which the correct answer is based.

MCP Exam Prerequisites

No exams or classes are required before you take the Designing and Implementing Databases with Microsoft SQL Server 2000 Enterprise Edition exam. However, in addition to the skills tested by the exam, you should have a working knowledge of the design and implementation of databases using SQL Server 2000. This knowledge should include:

- Logical database design
- Implementing physical databases, including creating and altering databases and database objects
- Retrieving and modifying data
- Programming business logic, including stored procedures, triggers, and transactions
- Tuning and optimizing queries and data access
- Designing a database security plan

Note After you have used the Readiness Review and determined that you are ready for the exam, use the Get More MCP Information link provided in the home page of the electronic assessment tool for information on scheduling for the exam. You can schedule exams up to six weeks in advance, or as late as one working day before the exam date.

Know the Products

Microsoft's certification program relies on exams that measure your ability to perform a specific job function or set of tasks. Microsoft develops the exams by analyzing the tasks performed by people who are currently working in the field. Therefore, the specific knowledge, skills, and abilities relating to the job are reflected in the certification exam.

Because the certification exams are based on real-world tasks, you need to gain hands-on experience with the applicable technology in order to master the exam. In a sense, you might consider hands-on experience in an organizational environment to be a prerequisite for passing an MCP exam. Many of the questions relate directly to Microsoft products or technology, so use opportunities at your organization or home to practice using the relevant tools.

Using the MCSE Readiness Review

Although you can use the Readiness Review in a number of ways, you might start your studies by taking the electronic assessment as a pretest. After completing the exam, review your results for each Objective Domain and focus your studies first on the Objective Domains for which you received the lowest scores. The electronic assessment allows you to print your results, and a printed report of how you fared can be useful when reviewing the exam material in this book.

After you have taken the Readiness Review electronic assessment, use the Readiness Review book to learn more about the Objective Domains that you find difficult and to find listings of appropriate study materials that might supplement your knowledge. By reviewing why the answers are correct or incorrect, you can determine whether you need to study the objective topics more.

You can also use the Readiness Review book to focus on the exact objectives that you need to master. Each objective in the book contains several questions that help you determine whether you understand the information related to that particular skill. The book is also designed for you to answer each question before reviewing the correct answer and answer choice explanations.

The best method to prepare for the MCP exam is to use the Readiness Review book in conjunction with the electronic assessment and other study materials. Thoroughly studying and practicing the material, combined with substantial real-world experience, can help you fully prepare for the MCP exam.

Understanding the Readiness Review Conventions

Before you start using the Readiness Review, it is important that you understand the terms and conventions used in the electronic assessment and book.

Question Numbering System

The Readiness Review electronic assessment and book contain reference numbers for each question. Understanding the numbering format will help you use the Readiness Review more effectively. When Microsoft creates the exams, the questions are grouped by job skills called *Objectives*. These Objectives are then organized by sections known as *Objective Domains*. Each question can be identified by the Objective Domain and the Objective it covers. The question numbers follow this format:

Test Number.Objective Domain.Objective.Question Number

For example, question number 70-229.02.01.003 means that this is question three (003) for the first Objective (01) in the second Objective Domain (02) of the Designing and Implementing Databases with Microsoft SQL Server 2000 Enterprise Edition exam (70-229). Refer to the "Exam Objectives Summary" section later in this introduction to locate the numbers associated with particular objectives. Each question is numbered based on its presentation in the printed book. You can use this numbering system to reference questions on the electronic assessment or in the Readiness Review book. Even though the questions in the book are organized by objective, questions in the electronic assessment and actual certification exam are presented in random order.

Notational Conventions

- Characters or commands that you type appear in **bold lowercase** type.
- Variable information and URLs are *italicized. Italic* is also used for book titles.
- Acronyms appear in FULL CAPITALS.

Notes

Text marked *Note* contains supplemental information.

Using the Readiness Review Electronic Assessment

The Readiness Review electronic assessment simulates the actual MCP exam. Each iteration of the electronic assessment consists of 50 questions covering all the objectives for the Designing and Implementing Databases with Microsoft SQL Server 2000 Enterprise Edition exam. (MCP certification exams consist of approximately 50 questions.) Just as you would in a real certification exam, you see questions from the objectives in random order during the practice test. Similar to the certification exam, the electronic assessment allows you to mark questions and review them after you finish the test.

To increase its value as a study aid, you can take the electronic assessment multiple times. Each time you are presented with a different set of questions in a revised order; however, some questions might be repeated.

If you have used one of the certification exam preparation tests available from Microsoft, the Readiness Review electronic assessment should look familiar. The difference is that this electronic assessment gives you the opportunity to learn as you take the exam.

Installing and Running the Electronic Assessment Software

Before you begin using the electronic assessment, you need to install the software. You need a computer with the following minimum configuration:

- Multimedia PC with a 75 MHz Pentium or higher processor
- 16 MB RAM for Microsoft Windows 95 or Windows 98, or
- 32 MB RAM for Windows NT, or
- 64 MB RAM for Windows 2000
- Microsoft Internet Explorer 5.01 or later
- 17 MB of available hard disk space (additional 70 MB minimum of hard disk space to install Internet Explorer 5.5 from this CD-ROM)
- A double-speed CD-ROM drive or better
- Super VGA display with at least 256 colors

► **To install the electronic assessment**

1. Insert the Readiness Review compact disc into your CD-ROM drive.

   A starting menu will display automatically, with links to the resources included on the CD-ROM.

Note If your system does not have Microsoft Internet Explorer 5.01 or later, you can install Internet Explorer 5.5 now by selecting the appropriate option on the menu.

---

2. Click Install Readiness Review.

   A dialog box appears, indicating you will install the MCSE Readiness Review on your computer.

3. Click Next.

   The License Agreement dialog box appears.

4. To continue with the installation of the electronic assessment engine, you must accept the License Agreement by clicking Yes.

5. The Choose Destination Location dialog box appears showing a default installation directory. Either accept the default or change the installation directory if needed. Click Next to copy the files to your hard drive.

6. A Question dialog box appears asking whether you would like Setup to create a desktop shortcut for this program. If you click Yes, an icon will be placed on your desktop.

7. The Setup Complete dialog box appears. Select whether you want to view the Readme.txt file after closing the Setup program, and then click Finish.

   The electronic assessment software is completely installed. If you chose to view the Readme.txt file, it will launch in a new window. For optimal viewing, enable word wrap.

► **To start the electronic assessment**

1. From the Start menu, point to Programs, point to MCSE Readiness Review, and then click MCSE RR Exam 70-229.

   The electronic assessment program starts.

2. Click Start Test.

   Information about the electronic assessment program appears.

3. Click OK.

Taking the Electronic Assessment

The Readiness Review electronic assessment consists of 50 multiple-choice questions, and as in the certification exam, you can skip questions or mark them for later review. Each exam question contains a question number that you can use to refer back to the Readiness Review book.

Before you end the electronic assessment, you should make sure to answer all the questions. When the exam is graded, unanswered questions are counted as incorrect and will lower your score. Similarly, on the actual certification exam you should complete all questions, or the unanswered ones will be counted as incorrect. No trick questions appear on the exam. The correct answer will always be among the list of choices. Some questions might have more than one correct answer, and this will be indicated in the question. A good strategy is to eliminate the most obvious incorrect answers first to make it easier for you to select the correct answer.

You have 75 minutes to complete the electronic assessment. During the exam you will see a timer indicating the amount of time you have remaining. This will help you to gauge the amount of time you should use to answer each question and to complete the exam. The amount of time you are given on the actual certification exam varies with each exam. Generally, certification exams take approximately 100 minutes to complete.

Ending and Grading the Electronic Assessment

When you click the Score Test button, you have the opportunity to review the questions you marked or left incomplete. (This format is not similar to the one used on the actual certification exam, in which you can verify whether you are satisfied with your answers and then click the Grade Test button.) The electronic assessment is graded when you click the Score Test button, and the software presents your section scores and your total score.

Note You can always end a test without grading your electronic assessment by clicking the Home button.

After your electronic assessment is graded, you can view the correct and incorrect answers by clicking the Review Questions button.

Interpreting the Electronic Assessment Results

The Score screen shows you the number of questions in each Objective Domain section, the number of questions you answered correctly, and a percentage grade for each section. You can use the Score screen to determine where to spend additional time studying. On the actual certification exam, the number of questions and passing score will depend on the exam you are taking. The electronic assessment records your score each time you grade an exam so that you can track your progress over time.

► **To view your progress and exam records**

1. From the electronic assessment Main menu, click View History. Each test attempt score appears.
2. Click a test attempt date/time to view your score for each objective domain.

   Review these scores to determine which Objective Domains you should study further. You can also use the scores to determine your progress.

Ordering More Questions

Self Test Software offers practice tests to help you prepare for a variety of MCP certification exams. These practice tests contain hundreds of additional questions and are similar to the Readiness Review electronic assessment. For a fee, you can order exam practice tests for this exam and other Microsoft certification exams. Click the Order More Questions link on the electronic assessment tool home page for more information.

Using the Readiness Review Book

You can use the Readiness Review book as a supplement to the Readiness Review electronic assessment, or as a standalone study aid. If you decide to use the book as a standalone study aid, review the Table of Contents or the list of objectives to find topics of interest or an appropriate starting point for you. To get the greatest benefit from the book, use the electronic assessment as a pretest to determine the Objective Domains for which you should spend the most study time. Or, if you would like to research specific questions while taking the electronic assessment, you can use the question number located on the question screen to reference the question number in the Readiness Review book.

One way to determine areas in which additional study might be helpful is to carefully review your individual section scores from the electronic assessment and note objective areas where your score could be improved. The section scores correlate to the Objective Domains listed in the Readiness Review book.

Reviewing the Objectives

Each Objective Domain in the book contains an introduction and a list of practice skills. Each list of practice skills describes suggested tasks you can perform to help you understand the objectives. Some of the tasks suggest reading additional material, whereas others are hands-on practices with software or hardware. You should pay particular attention to the hands-on practices because the certification exam reflects real-world knowledge you can gain only by working with the software or technology. Increasing your real-world experience with the relevant products and technologies will improve your performance on the exam.

Once you have chosen the objectives you would like to study, turn to the Table of Contents to locate the objectives in the Readiness Review book. You can study each objective separately, but you might need to understand the concepts explained in other objectives.

Make sure you understand the key terms for each objective. You will need a thorough understanding of these terms to answer the objective's questions correctly. Key term definitions are located in the Glossary of this book.

Reviewing the Questions

Each objective includes questions followed by the possible answers. After you review the question and select a probable answer, turn to the Answer section to determine whether you answered the question correctly. (For information about the question-numbering format, see "Question Numbering System," earlier in this introduction.)

The Readiness Review briefly discusses each possible answer and explains why each answer is correct or incorrect. After reviewing each explanation, if you feel you need more information about a topic, question, or answer, refer to the Further Reading section for that domain for more information.

The answers to the questions in the Readiness Review are based on current industry specifications and standards. However, the information provided by the answers is subject to change as technology improves and changes.

Exam Objectives Summary

The Designing and Implementing Databases with Microsoft SQL Server 2000 Enterprise Edition certification exam (70-229) measures your ability to implement, administer, and troubleshoot SQL Server 2000 Enterprise Edition.

Before taking the exam, you should be proficient with the job skills presented in the following sections. The sections provide the exam objectives and the corresponding objective numbers (which you can use to reference the questions in the Readiness Review electronic assessment and book) grouped by Objective Domains.

Objective Domain 1: Developing a Logical Data Model

The objectives in Objective Domain 1 are as follows:

- Objective 1.1 (70-229.01.01)—Define entities.
- Objective 1.2 (70-229.01.02)—Design entity keys.
- Objective 1.3 (70-229.01.03)—Design attribute domain integrity.

Objective Domain 2: Implementing the Physical Database

The objectives in Objective Domain 2 are as follows:

- Objective 2.1 (70-229.02.01)—Create and alter databases.
- Objective 2.2 (70-229.02.02)—Create and alter database objects.
- Objective 2.3 (70-229.02.03)—Alter database objects to support replication and partitioned views.
- Objective 2.4 (70-229.02.04)—Troubleshoot failed object creation.

Objective Domain 3: Retrieving and Modifying Data

The objectives in Objective Domain 3 are as follows:

- Objective 3.1 (70-229.03.01)—Import and export data.
- Objective 3.2 (70-229.03.02)—Manipulate heterogeneous data.
- Objective 3.3 (70-229.03.03)—Retrieve, filter, group, summarize, and modify data by using Transact-SQL.
- Objective 3.4 (70-229.03.04)—Manage result sets by using cursors and Transact-SQL.
- Objective 3.5 (70-229.03.05)—Extract data in XML format.

Objective Domain 4: Programming Business Logic

The objectives in Objective Domain 4 are as follows:

- Objective 4.1 (70-229.04.01)—Manage data manipulation by using stored procedures, transactions, triggers, user-defined functions, and views.
- Objective 4.2 (70-229.04.02)—Enforce procedural business logic by using stored procedures, transactions, triggers, user-defined functions, and views.
- Objective 4.3 (70-229.04.03)—Troubleshoot and optimize programming objects.

Objective Domain 5: Tuning and Optimizing Data Access

The objectives in Objective Domain 5 are as follows:

- Objective 5.1 (70-229.05.01)—Analyze the query execution plan.
- Objective 5.2 (70-229.05.02)—Capture, analyze, and replay SQL Profiler traces.
- Objective 5.3 (70-229.05.03)—Create and implement indexing strategies.
- Objective 5.4 (70-229.05.04)—Improve index use by using the Index Tuning Wizard.
- Objective 5.5 (70-229.05.05)—Monitor and troubleshoot database activity by using SQL Profiler.

Objective Domain 6: Designing a Database Security Plan

The objectives in Objective Domain 6 are as follows:

- Objective 6.1 (70-229.06.01)—Control data access by using stored procedures, triggers, user-defined functions, and views.
- Objective 6.2 (70-229.06.02)—Define object-level security including column-level permissions by using GRANT, REVOKE, and DENY.
- Objective 6.3 (70-229.06.03)—Create and manage application roles.

Getting More Help

A variety of resources are available to help you study for the exam. Your options include instructor-led classes, seminars, self-paced training kits, or other learning materials. The materials described here are created to prepare you for MCP exams. Each training resource fits a different type of learning style and budget.

Microsoft Official Curriculum (MOC)

Microsoft Official Curriculum (MOC) courses are technical training courses developed by Microsoft product groups to educate computer professionals who use Microsoft technology. The courses are developed with the same objectives used for Microsoft certification, and MOC courses are available to support most exams for the MCSE certification. The courses are available in instructor-led, online, or self-paced formats to fit your preferred learning style.

Self-Paced Training

Microsoft Press self-paced training kits cover a variety of Microsoft technical products. The self-paced kits are based on MOC courses, feature lessons, hands-on practices, multimedia presentations, practice files, and demonstration software. They can help you understand the concepts and get the experience you need to take the corresponding MCP exam.

To help you prepare for the Designing and Implementing Databases with Microsoft SQL Server 2000 (70-229) MCP exam, Microsoft has written the *Microsoft SQL Server 2000 System Administration* training kit. With this official self-paced training kit, you can learn the fundamentals of using SQL Server 2000. This kit gives you training for the real world by offering hands-on training through CD-ROM-based exercises.

MCP Approved Study Guides

MCP Approved Study Guides, available through several organizations, are learning tools that help you prepare for MCP exams. The study guides are available in a variety of formats to match your learning style, including books, compact discs, online content, and videos. These guides come in a wide range of prices to fit your budget.

Microsoft Seminar Series

Microsoft Solution Providers and other organizations are often a source of information to help you prepare for an MCP exam. For example, many solution providers will present seminars to help industry professionals understand a particular product technology, such as networking. For information on all Microsoft-sponsored events, visit *http://www.microsoft.com/events*.

OBJECTIVE DOMAIN 1

Developing a Logical Data Model

The Developing a Logical Data Model domain focuses on the skills required to build the foundation for any database system—the **logical data model**. This model is used to validate and document the business rules and functions of the database in a graphic manner.

The first step in developing the model consists of defining the pertinent business entities, determining the relationships between these entities, and identifying the **cardinality** of these relationships. Then the defining **attributes** are added to each entity, and the model is checked for **normalization**. Next the **primary keys** are determined, and through the relationships, the **foreign keys** are defined. Once the fundamental entity relationships are understood, attribute data types, **scale** and **precision**, allowed values, and **nullability** are determined. All of these steps are covered in this section of the exam.

Although any modeling tool can be used to create a logical model (especially because a logical model should be product-independent), Microsoft Visio, with its data modeling stencils, is an excellent modeling tool that can be used throughout the database design and implementation phases.

Tested Skills and Suggested Practices

The skills that you need to successfully master the Developing a Logical Data Model objective domain on the *Designing and Implementing Databases with Microsoft SQL Server 2000 Enterprise Edition* exam include:

- **Defining entities; considerations include entity composition and normalization.**
  - Practice 1: For this practice, create a list of all of the reasonable entities, with the entity name only, that would exist for a sample business function.

- Practice 2: Add the attributes that describe the entity.
- Practice 3: Validate that the model meets the three main requirements for normal form. Ensure that there are no repeating groups, that all of the attributes in an entity depend on the whole primary key, and that attributes depend only on the primary key and not on any other attributes.

- **Defining entity keys; considerations include primary keys, foreign keys, and unique constraints.**
  - Practice 1: Using the logical entity model created in the previous practice, determine the relationships between the entities, identifying the cardinality as one-to-one, one-to-many, or many-to-many. If your chosen design tool does not include the ability to model a many-to-many relationship, you can add an associative entity in between.
  - Practice 2: Evaluate your logical model for redundancies, circular relationships, and invalid assumptions. Determine whether all business objects are included. It is critical that this simple logical model be flexible, stable, and appropriate for the business function being modeled because it will provide the foundation for all remaining work on the project. Take the time to validate the relationships.
  - Practice 3: Determine all possible candidate keys for each entity and identify the primary keys. Add the primary key names to the models, as well as the corresponding foreign key names, based on the relationships already defined.

- **Defining attribute domain integrity; considerations include CHECK constraints, data types, and nullability.**
  - Practice 1: Determine the data types, including the scale and precision of each attribute, the allowable values, and the nullability of each attribute.
  - Practice 2: Validate the logical model against the business rules and functions and ensure that all possible requirements that can be met are met by the relational model. Keep in mind that businesses change over time, and it is not to your advantage to have to change the fundamentals of the model to include these types of business rules.

Further Reading

This section lists supplemental readings by objective. Study these sources thoroughly before taking exam 70-229.

Objective 1.1

Date, C. J. *An Introduction to Database Systems*. Reading, Mass.: Addison-Wesley, 1995. Review Chapter 4, "Relational Data Objects: Domains and Relations." This is the fundamental book about database systems.

Fleming, Candace C. and Barbara von Halle. *Handbook of Relational Database Design*. Reading, Mass.: Addison-Wesley, 1989. Review Chapter 5, "Build Skeletal User Views," in Part Two, "Building a Logical Data Model." This book is considered a classic for an introduction to relational design.

Elmasri, Ramez A. and Shamkant B. Navathe. *Fundamentals of Database Systems*. Reading, Mass.: Addison-Wesley, 1994. Review Chapter 3, "Data Modeling using the Entity-Relationship Approach," and Chapter 6, Section 1, "Relational Model Concepts." This book is fairly academic, but provides a concise description of the fundamentals.

Litwin, Paul. "Fundamentals of Relational Database Design." (This paper can be downloaded for free at *http://www.microsoft.com/TechNet*. You can find this paper by searching on the title.) Review the sections on relationships and normalization. This paper provides a good, short overview of relational database design.

Simsion, Graeme C. *Data Modeling Essentials: Analysis, Design, and Innovation*. Boston, Mass.: International Thompson Computer Press, 1993. Review Chapter 1, "What is Data Modeling?"; Chapter 2, "Basic Normalization"; Chapter 3, "The Entity Relationship Approach"; Chapter 6, "More About Relationships and Foreign Keys"; and Chapter 7, "Advanced Normalization." These chapters provide user-friendly descriptions of data modeling fundamentals.

Teorey, Toby J. *Database Modeling and Design*. San Francisco: Morgan Kaufmann, 1999. Review Chapter 3, "ER Modeling in Logical Database Design," and Chapter 5, "Normalization." These chapters provide user-friendly descriptions of data modeling fundamentals.

Microsoft SQL Server 2000 product documentation. To access Books Online (BOL), click the Start button, and point to Programs, then Microsoft SQL Server, and then Books Online. Click the Contents tab and double-click any of the following topics: "Database Design Considerations," "Creating a Database Plan," "Logical Database Modeling," and "Normalization." Although the BOL information about database design is limited, it is a good starting place.

Microsoft Corporation. *MCSE Training Kit: Microsoft SQL Server 2000 Database Design and Implementation*. Redmond, Washington: Microsoft Press, 2001. Read and complete the practices in Lessons 1 and 2 in Chapter 3, "Designing SQL Server Database."

Objective 1.2

Date, C. J. *An Introduction to Database Systems*. Reading, Mass.: Addison-Wesley, 1995. Review Chapter 5, "Relational Data Integrity: Candidate Keys and Related Matters."

Fleming, Candace C. and Barbara von Halle. *Handbook of Relational Database Design*. Reading, Mass.: Addison-Wesley, 1989. Review Chapter 6, "Add Keys to User Views," in Part Two, "Building a Logical Data Model."

Litwin, Paul. "Fundamentals of Relational Database Design." (This paper can be downloaded for free at *http://www.microsoft.com/TechNet*. You can find this paper by searching on the title.)

Simsion, Graeme C. *Data Modeling Essentials: Analysis, Design, and Innovation*. Boston, Mass.: International Thompson Computer Press, 1993. Review Chapter 8, "Primary Keys and Identity," and Chapter 9, "Attributes."

Microsoft SQL Server 2000 product documentation. To access Books Online, click the Start button, and point to Programs, then Microsoft SQL Server, and then Books Online. Click the Contents tab, double-click "Creating and Maintaining Databases," and review the following topics: "Primary Key Constraints," "Foreign Key Constraints," and "Unique Constraints."

Microsoft Corporation. *MCSE Training Kit: Microsoft SQL Server 2000 Database Design and Implementation*. Redmond, Washington: Microsoft Press, 2001. Read and complete the practices in Lessons 1 and 2 in Chapter 5, "Implementing Data Integrity."

Objective 1.3

Fleming, Candace C. and Barbara von Halle. *Handbook of Relational Database Design*. Reading, Mass.: Addison-Wesley, 1989. Review Chapter 9, "Determine Additional Attribute Business Rules," in Part Two, "Building a Logical Data Model."

Simsion, Graeme C. *Data Modeling Essentials: Analysis, Design, and Innovation*. Boston, Mass.: International Thompson Computer Press, 1993. Review Chapter 8, "Primary Keys and Identity," and Chapter 9, "Attributes."

Microsoft SQL Server 2000 product documentation. To access Books Online, click the Start button, and point to Programs, then Microsoft SQL Server, and then Books Online. Click the Contents tab and double-click the "Creating and Maintaining Databases" section. Review the "Data Integrity" topic.

Microsoft Corporation. *MCSE Training Kit: Microsoft SQL Server 2000 Database Design and Implementation*. Redmond, Washington: Microsoft Press, 2001. Read and complete the practices in Lessons 2 and 3 in Chapter 4, "Implementing SQL Server Databases and Tables," and Lessons 1 and 2 in Chapter 5, "Implementing Data Integrity."

OBJECTIVE 1.1

Define entities.

The first step to a well-designed database model to be implemented in SQL Server 2000 is to determine the valid entities for the model. Although this phase might seem simple at first glance—just a diagram of a group of boxes with titles in them—this phase is critical to the success of any dependent project. Changes to a logical model after development has begun, or worse, has been implemented, can have huge implications, much like a pebble thrown into a pond. The ripples affect every part of an organization's code, documentation, and users. It is critical to understand the business functions and their relationships at a deep and fundamental level. The logical model allows you to work your way to this understanding, by the iterative process of the modeling, discussion with the pertinent business and subject matter experts, and validation of the model.

This model must also be flexible and it should be considered as part of an enterprise data model. Although you might not be modeling the entire organization's data at this time, there is a very good chance that the model will need to be extended to a new area or incorporated with an independently designed model. It is to the organization's best advantage to ensure that the model adheres to fundamental modeling concepts and the enterprise perspective. Consider all of the code, documentation, training manuals, **stored procedures**, business objects and components, and so on that need to be changed if the basic logical model is flawed and invalid for the organization. The cost of such a change is huge, so the time spent getting it right at this point is worth the effort.

A well-designed data model must not only be valid for the business, but also it needs to be scalable, maintainable, and extensible. An elegant data model will encompass all of these attributes.

Many examples of "generic" data models have already been created, validated, and implemented that might fit your needs. Usually you will need to customize these, or slice off the particular parts that are pertinent to your project, but adhering to these common models will help to ensure extensibility.

The last critical piece to a logical data model is to ensure that the appropriate resources are available to help validate the model. This will need to include business people, who might have no understanding of databases, but who understand the business and its processes, and a database architect who can translate the business into a model.

After the entities have been determined, adding the attributes for the entities helps validate that the correct entity selections have been made. When the entities and their attributes have been designed, the model should be checked to verify that it meets at least the first three levels of normal form. These levels are

- No repeating groups or multivalue attributes.
- Every attribute in the entity must be dependent on the whole primary key.
- Every attribute in the entity must be dependent only on the primary key.

You can easily remember the last two by the following saying: "All attributes must be dependent on the key, the whole key, and nothing but the key."

Objective 1.1 Questions

70-229.01.01.001

You design the following entities for a school course system. You would like to normalize the entities. What should you do?

Examine the entities shown here.

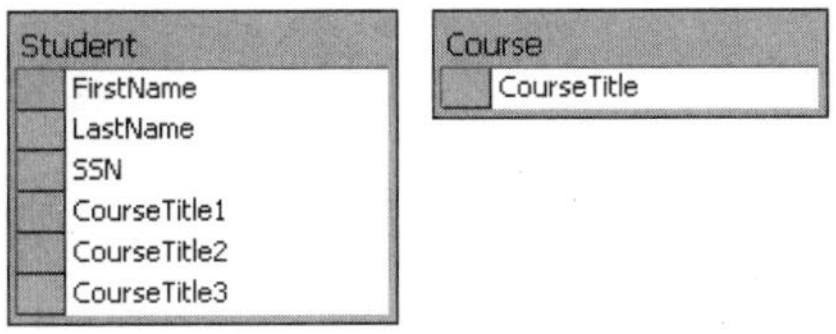

A. Remove the CourseTitle1, CourseTitle2, and CourseTitle3 attributes in the Student entity.

B. Remove the Course entity.

C. Add enough CourseTitle attributes in the Student entity to accommodate all of the courses that a student might take.

70-229.01.01.002

You have created a model with two entities for a school course system. You would like to normalize the entities. What should you do?

Examine the entities shown here.

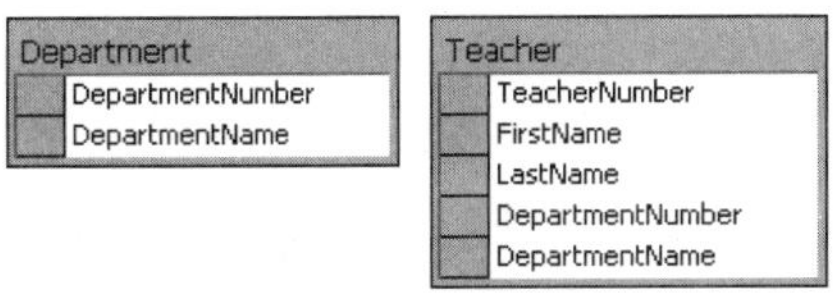

A. Add a TeacherNumber to the Department entity.

B. Replace the FirstName and LastName attributes in the Teacher entity with TeacherName.

C. Remove the DepartmentName from the Teacher entity.

70-229.01.01.003

You design a logical model for current enrollment in a university. You want to remove any redundant attributes or derived attributes that are dependent on other attributes. What should you do?

Examine the entities shown here.

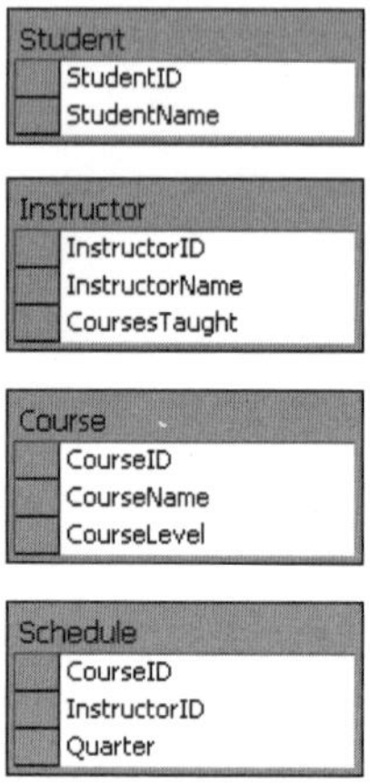

A. Remove the InstructorID from the Schedule entity.

B. Remove the CoursesTaught attribute from the Instructor entity.

C. Remove the CourseName from the Course entity.

D. Remove the CourseID from the Schedule entity.

70-229.01.01.004

You are designing a logical model to track airline flights. In your system, an airplane is owned by one airline, and a flight would always be flown by one airplane. You create the following entities:

- Airplane
- Flight
- Airline

In the following sentence diagrams, the arrows indicate a one-to-many relationship. Which of the following diagrams describes the relationship between these three entities that meets the scenario requirements?

A. Flight → Airline → Airplane

B. Airplane → Airline → Flight

C. Airplane → Flight → Airline

D. Airline → Airplane → Flight

Objective 1.1 Answers

70-229.01.01.001

▶ Correct Answers: A

A. **Correct:** The multiple CourseTitle attributes are an example of repeating groups, and are a violation of first normal form. This will obviously waste space and is inflexible.

B. **Incorrect:** The Course entity will be needed. Removing it will do nothing to normalize the Student entity, and the CourseTitle attributes are still left as repeating groups.

C. **Incorrect:** This proposed solution is a violation of first normal form, in that there are repeating groups. This causes many problems, including wasted space, and is very difficult to program against.

70-229.01.01.002

▶ Correct Answers: C

A. **Incorrect:** The TeacherNumber is not part of the Department entity and does not describe the Department entity in any way, but rather describes the Teacher.

B. **Incorrect:** Combining the names does not address any normalization problems. It does not remove repeating groups.

C. **Correct:** The DepartmentName is dependent on the DepartmentNumber and anything that would be considered a primary key for a Teacher. Leaving this in can cause data inconsistency in that a change to a DepartmentName will require not only a change to the Department entity, but also to all of the Teacher rows that have the same name.

70-229.01.01.003

▶ Correct Answers: B

A. **Incorrect:** The InstructorID is part of the primary key of the Schedule entity and it is required to describe a Schedule instance. It is not a derived attribute, and it is not redundant because it is also a foreign key reference to the Instructor entity.

B. **Correct:** This attribute would need to be derived from a calculation based on the count for a teacher in the Schedule entity. This derived data would also be redundant and could lead to data inconsistencies if this attribute were changed without a change to the instances in the Schedule entity.

C. **Incorrect:** The CourseName is not redundant or derived; it is a description that is required for the Course entity.

D. **Incorrect:** The CourseID is part of the primary key for the Schedule entity. It is not derived, and it is not redundant because it is also a foreign key reference to the Course entity.

70-229.01.01.004

► Correct Answers: D

A. **Incorrect:** In this model, an airplane would have one foreign key reference to an airline, and an airline would have many airplanes. This is correct. However, the model shows an airline as having a foreign key relationship with a flight, which is not correct as described by the scenario. There would not be any way to determine what airplane was assigned to a flight.

B. **Incorrect:** In this model, there is a one-to-many relationship between an airplane and an airline. This is not correct because we know from the scenario that an airplane is owned by one airline. Also, in this model one airline would have many flights. Although this is correct, the relationship between an airline and a flight should be tracked through the airplane, not directly through the airline.

C. **Incorrect:** Here one airplane is allowed per flight, which is correct. However, one flight is allowed per airline, and that is obviously not accurate because an airline would have many flights.

D. **Correct:** Here one airline is allowed per airplane, and many airplanes per airline, which follows the scenario requirement that an airplane is owned by one airline. There is one airplane per flight, and many flights per airplane, which is again correct. We know that a flight is flown by only one plane.

OBJECTIVE 1.2

Design entity keys.

This section of the exam focuses on identifying the **primary keys**, **foreign keys**, and any **unique constraints**.

The first step to identifying entity keys is to determine all possible candidates for the primary key. These are any attributes, or combination of attributes, that can uniquely identify an instance of the entity, or a row. There might be more than one candidate for selection as the primary key, and each one of these possibilities needs to be identified. In collaboration with the business, a determination of the most appropriate candidate is selected as the primary key.

There are three major considerations for a primary key. A primary key should be:

- Applicable
- Minimal
- Stable

An applicable primary key simply means that this is the best selection for uniquely identifying each instance in this entity.

A minimal key means that it is as small as possible because it might be heavily used throughout the model, and subsequently the database. The combination of a customer name, address, and phone number is not a good example of a minimal primary key.

A stable primary key means that the possibility of the value changing is very small. In general, it is best not to change a primary key because if it is part of a relationship, the value will need to be migrated throughout the system. This can have a large impact.

Although every entity must, by definition, have a candidate for a primary key, it is quite common to use a system-generated key, called a **surrogate key**, as the primary key. An example of this is a people entity. A true unique identifier for a person is a large combination of many things, and it might not actually exist at all, so a unique key that has no meaning outside of the system is generated.

After a primary key is determined for each entity, this key is migrated to every entity that has a foreign key reference to it. The key can be renamed to be better understood in the context of the referring entity, but it must have the same data type.

Lastly, every candidate primary key that is not selected as the actual primary key, including attribute combinations, must have a unique constraint to enforce the logical candidate. For example, although you might decide to create a surrogate key called Country Code for a Country entity, and designate this as the primary key, the Country Name is a candidate key and could also have been selected as the primary key. It should, therefore, have a unique constraint to enforce this.

Objective 1.2 Questions

70-229.01.02.001

You are creating a database to track music compositions submitted for copyright to a large international copyright company. Copyrights might be acquired for every composition submitted, but a particular composer can submit only one composition of the same name at any time. You create a composer entity with a composer ID for the primary key. You also create a composition entity. Which of the following provides the best logical primary key for each row in the composition entity?

A. Composition name

B. Composition name and composition year

C. Composition name and composer ID

D. Composition name and copyright number

70-229.01.02.002

You are designing a data model to track software projects. A project might be undertaken in one department or in multiple departments. Each project is assigned a group of programmers. A programmer who is a staff member of one department might also be assigned to a project that is being undertaken by another department, and a programmer might perform multiple jobs on a particular project. You design the model with the foreign key relationships as follows. Which of the following is true? (Choose all that apply.)

Examine the following logical model.

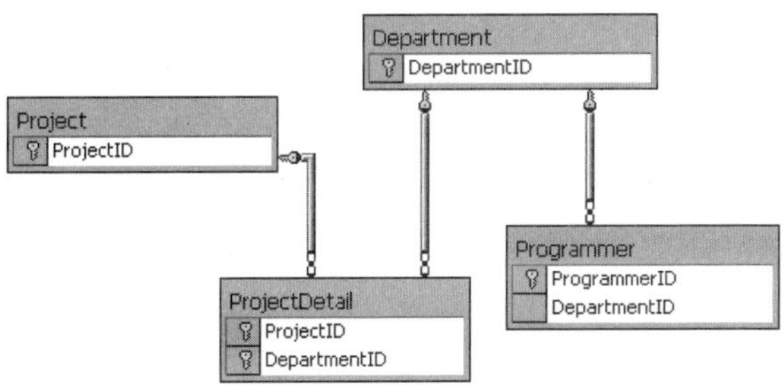

A. The programmers on each project can be determined.

B. The programmers on staff in each department can be determined.

C. The job being performed by a programmer on a project can be determined.

D. The projects being performed in a department can be determined.

70-229.01.02.003

You are creating a model to track employee reviews. Reviews are currently held at six-month intervals, and only one reviewer performs an employee's review. You create an employee entity and the following review entity. Which attributes would determine the uniqueness of a review?

Examine the Review Entity shown here.

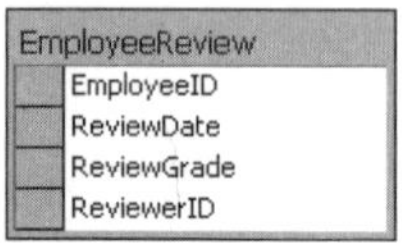

A. EmployeeID

B. EmployeeID, ReviewDate

C. EmployeeID, ReviewerID

D. EmployeeID, ReviewDate, ReviewGrade

70-229.01.02.004

You are creating a model of employees in a large international company. Each country provides a government-generated number given to every person authorized to work. Other information contained in the employee entity would be family name, given name, phone number, and address. Which of the following is the best choice to uniquely identify each employee?

A. Family name and given name

B. Government number

C. Family name, given name, phone number, and address

D. System-generated identity number

70-229.01.02.005

You are designing a logical model for museum art collections. You have currently designed Museum, Artist, and ArtObject entities. You want to accomplish the following results:

- Museums can be recognized as being part of a larger museum.
- The museum owning artwork created by a particular artist can be known.
- An art object that was created by more than one artist can be stored.
- A surrogate key can be used as the primary key for the museum.
- No museum can have the same name as another museum.

You perform the following actions:

- You add a one-to-many relationship between the Artist and ArtObject entities.
- You add a surrogate primary key attribute called MuseumID to the Museum entity.
- You add an attribute called ParentMuseumID and a self-referencing foreign key relationship to the Museum entity.
- You add a surrogate primary key attribute called ArtistID to the Artist table.
- You add a foreign key relationship between the ArtObject and the Museum entities.

Which of the results do these actions produce? (Choose all that apply.)

A. You ensure that museums can be recognized as being part of a larger museum.

B. You ensure that the museum holding artwork created by a particular artist can be known.

C. You ensure that an art object that was created by more than one artist can be stored.

D. You use a surrogate key for the primary key for the museum.

E. You ensure that no museum can have the same name as another museum.

70-229.01.02.006

You are creating a logical data model for tracking grants to nonprofit organizations for your company. Some organizations are part of another organization. Grants can be split between organizations. You need to be able to track how much money was given to any particular organization at any level. You design the model with the foreign key relationships as follows. Which of the following is true? (Choose all that apply.)

Examine the following logical model.

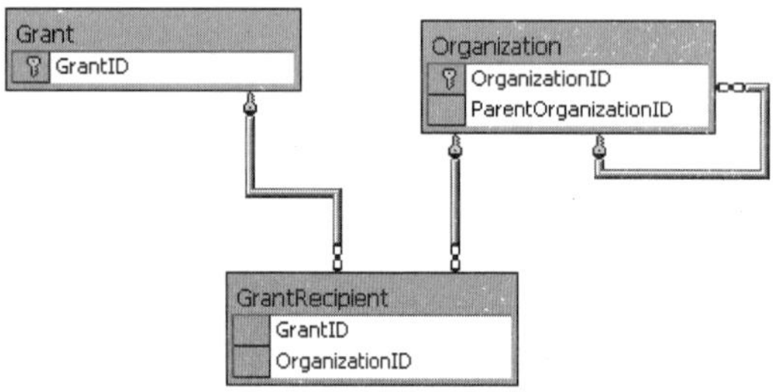

A. You are able to determine all of the organizations that are part of any particular parent organization.

B. Grants that are awarded to any organization can be determined, including any organizations for which it is considered a parent organization.

C. The organization that awards the grant can be determined.

Objective 1.2 Answers

70-229.01.02.001

▸ Correct Answers: C

A. **Incorrect:** Selecting composition name for the primary key would not allow submission of more than one composition with the same name. Although this might be rare, it would not be impossible.

B. **Incorrect:** Selecting composition name and composition year would allow for more than one composition of the same name to be submitted in the same year, but in this case, composition year is an arbitrary selection that is not indicated by any of the given business criteria. Again, more than one composition of the same name by different composers would not be allowed for submission in the same year.

C. **Correct:** Selecting composition name and composer ID provides the best candidate key for the scenario. It allows submission of compositions with the same names, but only one per composer.

D. **Incorrect:** This selection has two obvious problems. One is that a copyright number is not known at all times, and primary keys cannot be null. Also, if the copyright number were known, it would be assumed to be unique in itself, and a composition name would not be needed as well to uniquely identify a row in the entity.

70-229.01.02.002

▸ Correct Answers: B and D

A. **Incorrect:** Although the foreign key relationships in the model describe which department a programmer is part of, they do not allow us to determine which project the programmer is working on.

B. **Correct:** The model allows us to determine the programmers in each department because there is a foreign key in the Programmer entity that references the Department entity.

C. **Incorrect:** There is no information about a specific job in the model.

D. **Correct:** Because the ProjectDetail entity contains a foreign key to the Department entity, projects being performed in a department can be determined.

70-229.01.02.003

► Correct Answers: B

A. **Incorrect:** Selecting only EmployeeID as the primary key allows only one review per employee. This is not the correct primary key for this entity because the requirement is for employees to have multiple reviews.

B. **Correct:** The combination of EmployeeID and ReviewDate uniquely identifies an instance of a review for an employee. Although the scenario states that reviews are currently held at six-month intervals, the combination of the two attributes allows for this, as well as any other review interval. This makes this selection flexible. It also prohibits more than one reviewer per employee review.

C. **Incorrect:** Selecting the combination of EmployeeID and ReviewerID allows only one review per employee and reviewer combination. An employee could be reviewed more than once by the same reviewer, which this selection would prohibit.

D. **Incorrect:** There is no need to include the ReviewGrade in the primary key. This allows for multiple reviews on the same date for an employee, if there were different ReviewGrades. This is not the situation described in the scenario.

70-229.01.02.004

► Correct Answers: D

A. **Incorrect:** The selection of family name and given name for a primary key will not uniquely identify an employee because there can be many people with the same name within a large company. This selection also has one other problem, it does not meet the stability requirement for a good primary key. In many countries names change over time according to marital status. Every attempt should be made to ensure that primary keys do not change.

B. **Incorrect:** Although this might seem to be a good solution, there is no guarantee that these numbers are not recycled when a previous person has passed on (this is the case with Social Security numbers in the United States). Also, there is no guarantee that a number given out by one country will be unique in the world, or that there is a common type for these numbers (that is, numeric versus alphanumeric).

C. **Incorrect:** Although the chances are small that more than one person with the same name would have the same address and phone number, this is not impossible. (Consider George Forman and his sons, George, George, George, George, and George.) This selection does not uniquely identify an employee because the same person can be entered into the table with a different address. This selection also suffers from the instability problem and is simply too much data to use as a primary key, where the same data would need to be migrated to any tables that would refer to this entity.

D. **Correct:** Because there does not appear to be a simple, applicable, and stable candidate for a unique identifier for this entity, the best option is to create a unique number, generated by the system.

70-229.01.02.005

► Correct Answers: A, B, and D

A. **Correct:** By adding an attribute called ParentMuseumID and creating a self-referencing foreign key relationship to the Museum entity, you ensure that any museum can have another museum as a parent. This implementation allows only hierarchical relationships, and allows a museum to have only one parental museum.

B. **Correct:** Because there is a relationship between the Artist and ArtObject entities, and a relationship between the ArtObject and Museum entities, the museum that is holding artwork by a particular artist can be determined through these relationships.

C. **Incorrect:** Because there is only a one-to-many relationship between the Artist and ArtObject entities, there can only be one Artist associated with a particular ArtObject. To accomplish this result, a many-to-many relationship would need to be created and, in SQL Server 2000, this would require an associated table with a row for each Artist for an ArtObject.

D. **Correct:** Adding the MuseumID attribute to the Museum entity and then defining this attribute as the primary key produces this result.

E. **Incorrect:** There is nothing in the listed actions that ensures that only one museum has a particular name. The primary key, which will be unique by definition, has been defined on the surrogate key. A unique constraint will need to be added to the Museum name to produce this result. Whenever a surrogate key is used in an entity definition, it is important to also add any required unique constraints on candidate keys; otherwise, duplicate data can be entered.

70-229.01.02.006

▶ Correct Answers: A and B

A. **Correct:** The self-referencing foreign key relationship on Organization allows for all child organizations of a parent organization to be known.

B. **Correct:** Because there is a many-to-many relationship between the Organization entity and the Grant entity, all grants awarded to an institution can be determined through the GrantRecipient entity. Grants can also be summarized for parent organizations because of the self-referencing relationship on Organization.

C. **Incorrect:** This information is not contained in the model because the only relationship between an Organization and a Grant is through the GrantRecipient entity.

OBJECTIVE 1.3

Design attribute domain integrity.

Determining the **domain integrity** for an attribute can include determining the data type, nullability, and other constraints on the attribute. Determining attribute domains ensures that only the allowable values can be entered into the database. This includes whether alphanumeric or numeric data is allowed, whether a value can be null, and any other type of constraint or rule on the data, such as a range of allowable values.

Generally, determining a data type is straightforward. Discussions with the business about current and future possible values usually lead to accurate data type evaluations. The same is true for range constraints and other check constraints. Consistency in data type selection is important and can prevent problems later in the development process.

However, determining whether an attribute can be null is more problematic. Excessive usage of nulls can lead to difficulties in programming because SQL queries must be written differently when a null is expected. Any expression that contains a null will evaluate as unknown.

The question of whether nulls should be used in a relational database is fairly controversial. Because the use of nulls requires a three-valued logic that not all developers are aware of, you might find that to help ensure accuracy in your systems, you need to limit null usage. The following tables show the three-valued logic truth tables.

AND	True	False	Unknown
True	True	False	Unknown
False	False	False	False
Unknown	Unknown	False	Unknown

OR	True	False	Unknown
True	True	True	True
False	True	False	Unknown
Unknown	True	Unknown	Unknown

NOT	True	False	Unknown
	False	True	Unknown

In general, it is best to use nulls very sparingly, and as little as possible for any attribute that participates in a relationship. One good practice is to allow nulls only in descriptive text attributes. Some people use codes to represent the different types of nulls. For example, some attributes need to be null because they might not be applicable in every case; or the attribute value is not known at the moment, but can be considered required later; or the attribute value truly is not known. Using a code to represent these three "null states" can help with data integrity and data cleaning.

Objective 1.3 Questions

70-229.01.03.001

Evaluate the Customer and Repair entities shown below. A customer with an order should not be deleted. How should you enforce a relationship between the Customer and Repair entities to ensure integrity?

Examine the following logical model.

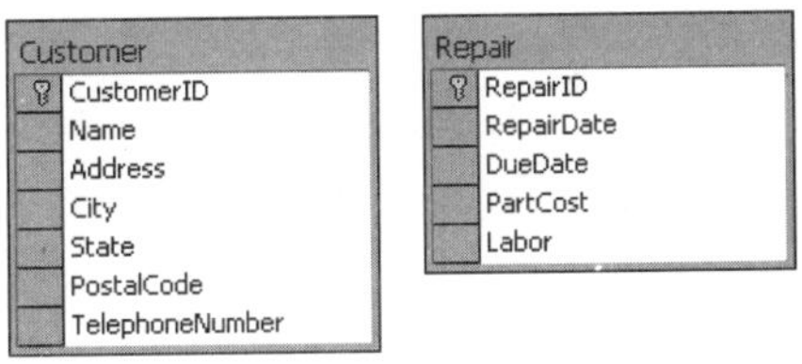

A. Add a CHECK constraint to the RepairID attribute.

B. Add a CHECK constraint to the CustomerID attribute.

C. Add a DELETE trigger to the Repair entity.

D. Add the CustomerID attribute to the Repair entity with a FOREIGN KEY constraint to the Customer entity.

70-229.01.03.002

You have to enforce relationships between the entities shown below. Telephone sales agents are compensated according to the number of customer calls and the duration of the time spent on the phone talking to customers. The agents are using different extensions as they move around. How would you enforce the relationship between the Agent records and the CallDetails to calculate commissions?

Examine the following logical model.

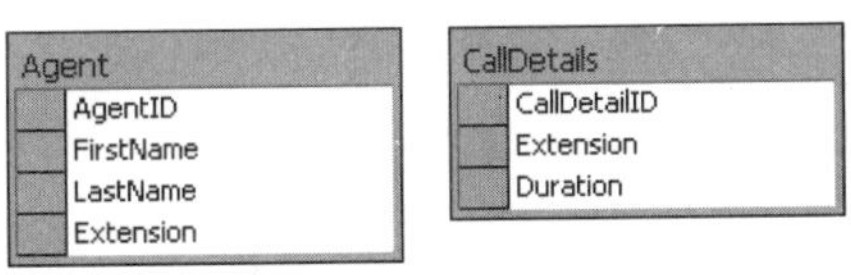

A. Add a FOREIGN KEY constraint on the Extension attribute in CallDetails referencing the Agent entity.

B. Create a procedure to query the Agent and CallDetails entities to determine the commissions.

C. Add AgentID to the CallDetails entity and create a FOREIGN KEY constraint referencing the Agent entity.

70-229.01.03.003

You are developing a database model for a high school. Evaluate the Student and State entities below. What should you change in the model to maintain data integrity?

Examine the following logical model.

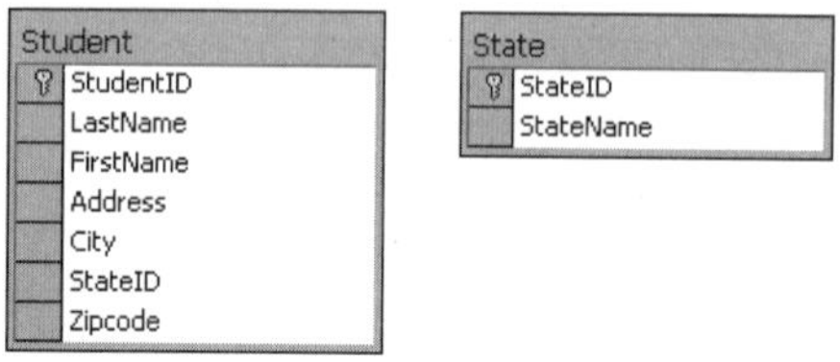

A. Add a FOREIGN KEY constraint to the Student entity referencing the State entity's StateID attribute.

B. Add a CHECK constraint to the State entity on the StateID attribute.

C. Add a CHECK constraint to the Student entity on the StateID attribute.

D. Add a FOREIGN KEY constraint to the State entity referencing the Student entity's StateID attribute.

70-229.01.03.004

You are building a rent-a-car tracing program. Evaluate the Customers, Agreements, and Cars entities shown below. Each customer can rent one or more cars. Each car can be rented to only one customer at a time. A car not owned by the rent-a-car office cannot be rented. How should you enforce integrity between the Agreements and Cars entities?

Examine the following logical model.

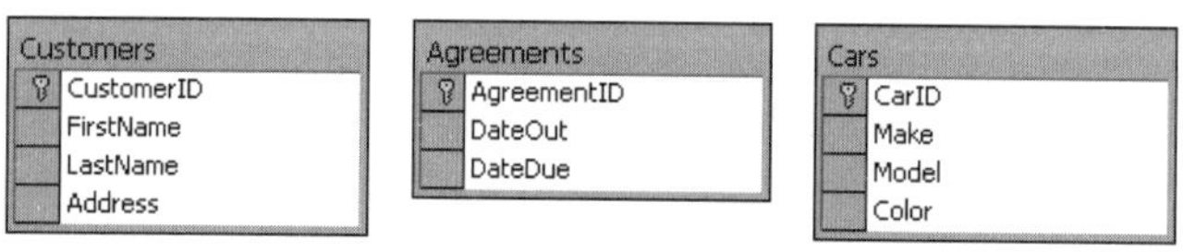

A. Add a CHECK constraint to the AgreementID attribute.

B. Add the AgreementID attribute to the Cars entity with a FOREIGN KEY constraint referencing the Agreements entity.

C. Add an INSERT trigger to the rental entity.

D. Add the CarID attribute to the Agreements entity with a FOREIGN KEY constraint referencing the Cars entity.

70-229.01.03.005

You have designed an entity for tracking orders and have added all of the attributes, including one called UnitPrice that will be used to store the actual price charged per product. Which data types and nullability should be set for the UnitPrice attribute to ensure that the results of any mathematical functions on UnitPrice will always be accurate?

A. A nullable integer.

B. A nullable float.

C. A nullable money.

D. A non-nullable integer.

E. A non-nullable float.

F. A non-nullable money.

70-229.01.03.006

You are designing a logical model to collect information about the composition of fragrances for perfumeries. This model will be used to create a database containing the recipes for different fragrances, and the percentages of each ingredient in the fragrance recipe will need to be tracked. You design an entity called PerfumeComposition and an entity called Ingredient. The percentage of each ingredient in a particular perfume will be stored in the PerfumeComposition table, one row for each ingredient. You want to ensure that the sum of the ingredient percentages for a perfume does not exceed 100. How can you accomplish this?

A. Add a CHECK constraint to the PerfumeComposition table that would disallow percentages of more than 100 per cent for a perfume.

B. Add a trigger to the PerfumeComposition table that would reject any percentage that would cause the sum of all of the percentages for a perfume to exceed 100 per cent.

C. Create a procedure to calculate any offending percentage every night and to delete the rows from the PerfumeComposition table.

D. Add a unique constraint to the percentage attribute in the PerfumeComposition table to disallow rows with the same percentages.

Objective 1.3 Answers

70-229.01.03.001

► Correct Answers: D

A. **Incorrect:** A CHECK constraint enforces strict values that can be stored in an attribute. A constraint contains a logical expression that must be evaluated before an INSERT into an attribute. Having a CHECK constraint could enforce some logical expression on the RepairID but would not prevent deletion of a customer.

B. **Incorrect:** Using a CHECK constraint on the CustomerID could enforce other rules on the CustomerID attribute but would not prevent the deletion of a customer.

C. **Incorrect:** A DELETE trigger is a stored procedure executed each time you delete a record from the Repair entity. This trigger would execute when you delete a record on the Repair entity but would not prevent a deletion of a record from the Customer entity.

D. **Correct:** You can add a CustomerID attribute to the Repair entity and configure it to have a FOREIGN KEY constraint referencing the Customer entity. You cannot delete a record from the referenced entity if you still have rows in the referencing entity. In this case, the Repair entity references the Customer entity, and rows cannot be deleted from the Customer entity until they are deleted first from the Repair entity.

70-229.01.03.002

► Correct Answers: C

A. **Incorrect:** Although the attribute referencing the agents by extension would be sufficient if they could not use more than one extension, the Extension attribute cannot be used correctly. You could associate agents with calls they did not make.

B. **Incorrect:** You cannot query the CallDetails and Agents entities to arrive at a commission because there is nothing to associate the two entities with each other. The Extension attribute cannot be used because the agents can use multiple extensions. You cannot tell who used the phone at that extension without adding an AgentID attribute to the CallDetails entity.

C. **Correct:** Adding the AgentID to the CallDetails entity and then creating the FOREIGN KEY constraint referencing the Agent entity is the correct relationship as described by the scenario.

70-229.01.03.003

▶ Correct Answers: A

A. **Correct:** Using a FOREIGN KEY constraint will guarantee data validity and guarantee that records cannot be deleted from the State entity while records referencing them exist in the Student entity.

B. **Incorrect:** A CHECK constraint can verify the validity of the new value. In this example you need to make sure that you cannot insert a student record without the correct StateID. A CHECK constraint placed on the State entity will validate data in the State entity but not in the Student entity. It will not guarantee data integrity between the two entities.

C. **Incorrect:** Although a CHECK constraint can determine which data can be placed in the Student entity based on the State entity, it does not stop deletion of records from the State entity.

D. **Incorrect:** A FOREIGN KEY constraint is correct, but the constraint should be placed on the Student entity referencing the State entity, not the other way around.

70-229.01.03.004

▶ Correct Answers: D

A. **Incorrect:** A CHECK constraint enforces domain integrity by restricting the values that can be entered into an attribute. A CHECK constraint contains a logical expression that must be true in order to accept the new value. A CHECK constraint on the AgreementID attribute would not enforce integrity between the Agreements entity and the Cars entity.

B. **Incorrect:** If a car could be rented only once, you could add the AgreementID to the Cars entity. Because a car can be rented many times, this will not work.

C. **Incorrect:** An INSERT trigger is a stored procedure that is executed automatically whenever you try to insert a record into the entity. A trigger can include most Transact-SQL (T-SQL) statements. Although a trigger could be placed on the Agreements entity to roll back the transaction if a car that is being rented is not in stock, a trigger should be used only when a constraint does not provide the necessary functionality.

D. **Correct:** You can add a CarID attribute to the Agreements entity and configure that attribute as a foreign key. This process enforces integrity between the Agreements entity and the Cars entity.

70-229.01.03.005

► Correct Answers: F

A. **Incorrect:** An integer is not the appropriate data type for UnitPrice because a price requires decimals. UnitPrice should also be non-nullable because a price is always known. It might have a UnitPrice of zero, but it would not be an unknown value.

B. **Incorrect:** A float is not the appropriate data type for UnitPrice because float data types are approximate and can have rounding errors in calculations, something that is frowned upon in money transactions. UnitPrice should also be non-nullable because a price is always known. It may have a UnitPrice of zero, but it would not be an unknown value.

C. **Incorrect:** Money is the correct data type for UnitPrice. This data type was designed specifically for monetary data, and it will not have the rounding problems that a float data type will exhibit. However, UnitPrice should be non-nullable because a price is always known. It may have a UnitPrice of zero, but it would not be an unknown value.

D. **Incorrect:** An integer would not be the appropriate data type for UnitPrice because a price will require decimals. However, UnitPrice should be non-nullable because a price is always known.

E. **Incorrect:** A float would not be the appropriate data type for UnitPrice because float data types are approximate and can have rounding errors in calculations, something that is frowned upon in money transactions. However, UnitPrice should be non-nullable because a price is always known.

F. **Correct:** Money is the correct data type for UnitPrice. This data type was designed specifically for monetary data, so it will not have the rounding problems that a float data type will exhibit. UnitPrice should also be non-nullable because a price is always known. It may have a UnitPrice of zero, but it would not be an unknown value. This combination is correct for the business function and rules required by the question.

70-229.01.03.006

▶ Correct Answers: B

A. **Incorrect:** It would not be possible to add a CHECK constraint to check across rows, summing the percentage.

B. **Correct:** This is the only way to implement this business rule in the database.

C. **Incorrect:** It is best not to change data after it has been entered, but rather to disallow its entry in the first place if it is incorrect. Deleting offending rows is a dangerous strategy because data would quickly become incorrect and invalid.

D. **Incorrect:** This does not address the sum of the rows in the PerfumeComposition table for a particular perfume exceeding 100 per cent.

OBJECTIVE DOMAIN 2

Implementing the Physical Database

The **physical database design** maps the **logical database design** to a physical medium. To develop a physical database design, you must take the available hardware into consideration. You need to take advantage of the available hardware and keep in mind the extensibility options of the existing or new hardware. Consider how the data will be accessed throughout the hardware system. The physical design addresses how data will be accessed, whereas the logical design models your business requirements and data. Physical design tends to be very platform-specific.

A well-designed database model is key to a successful high-performance database with efficient storage and retrieval of data. The design should be carefully reviewed to assess its impact on the database. You have to take a close look at the following aspects of database operations: performance, maintainability, extensibility, scalability, availability, and security.

Performance involves not just the response time of the query but the network traffic, disk I/O, and CPU utilization.

Maintainability involves the ongoing maintenance of the database, which includes backups and restores, rebuilding and creating new indexes, updating constraints, or partitioning data.

Extensibility refers to the ability to extend new functionality built into Microsoft SQL Server 2000 and future releases. It includes the extensibility of your database design to support future releases of your software.

Scalability refers to the ability to accommodate growing databases and numbers of new users without suffering performance hits or a breakdown.

Availability involves users, application servers, or other server processes to access the data in the database. Availability is measured in system uptime and has become more and more important in current Internet commerce systems.

Security refers to the control of access in the database and determination of who can access specific data in the database.

If you intend to implement a partitioned database at some time, this is the time to determine how that implementation could be done.

You should know how a logical database design could impact database performance. You need to have a firm understanding of the key terms in the following section to successfully answer the questions.

Tested Skills and Suggested Practices

The skills that you need to successfully master the Implementing the Physical Database objective domain on the *Designing and Implementing Databases with Microsoft SQL Server 2000 Enterprise Edition* exam include:

- **Evaluating the logical database and its impact on each aspect of database operations, such as performance, maintainability, extensibility, scalability, availability, security, and partitionability.**
  - Practice 1: For this practice you must use a logical database design. Collect all tables, views, indexes, constraints, and so on. List each feature of your design. List the number of tables, views, constraints, and so on. You should know the number of projected users, the estimated database size, and the anticipated database growth. Consider the hardware and whether it is expandable to grow with your business needs. Look at each item and determine the impact on the database. For example, more triggers can dramatically impact performance. Overly complex or too many indexes can do more harm than good.
  - Practice 2: Make a list of the critical standards of database quality, such as performance, maintainability, extensibility, scalability, availability, and security. Determine how each of these items impacts your standard of database quality.
  - Practice 3: Look closely at how normalization and denormalization would affect your standard of database quality.
- **Modifying a logical database design to minimize its impact on database operations.**
  - Practice 1: Review the list you created for the first practice and take a look at what part of your database design you would change to improve maintainability. For example, you might want to limit the number of indexes or the size of the database. You might find that your database is already designed to support maximum maintainability and you do not need to make any changes.
  - Practice 2: You need to take into consideration the performance of your database and decide whether you need to make changes in your logical database design to improve performance. You might need to rework some joins, denormalize some tables, or introduce new indexes.

- Practice 3: Based on the list you have created, look at the availability of the database design. You might consider consolidating your databases or introducing partitioning.

- **Determining the impact that database design modifications will have on database operations.**
  - Practice 1: Add a denormalized table to your database. Make sure you add the necessary indexes, triggers, views, and constraints. Look at the impact the denormalized table had on the performance and size of database operation.
  - Practice 2: Add views to your database to see how they impact the aspects of the database.
  - Practice 3: Expand the database with extra data to see how the expansion affects your database.

Further Reading

This section lists supplemental readings by objective. Study these sources thoroughly before taking exam 70-229.

Objective 2.1

Microsoft SQL Server 2000 product documentation. To access Books Online, click the Start button, point to Programs, then Microsoft SQL Server, and then click Books Online. Click the Contents tab, double-click "Creating and Maintaining Databases," and review "Databases," "Database Design Considerations," "Creating a Database," and "Optimizing Database Performance."

Delaney, Kalen. *Inside Microsoft SQL Server 2000*. Redmond, Washington: Microsoft Press, 2000. Review Chapter 5, "Databases and Database Files."

Microsoft Corporation. *MCSE Training Kit: Microsoft SQL Server 2000 Database Design and Implementation*. Redmond, Washington: Microsoft Press, 2001. Read and complete the practices in Lessons 1, 2, and 3 in Chapter 3, "Designing SQL Server Database," and Lesson 1 in Chapter 4, "Implementing SQL Server Databases and Tables."

Objective 2.2

Microsoft SQL Server 2000 product documentation. To access Books Online, click the Start button, point to Programs, then Microsoft SQL Server, and then click Books Online. Click the Contents tab, double-click "Creating and Maintaining Databases," and review "Tables" and "Views."

Delaney, Kalen. *Inside Microsoft SQL Server 2000*. Redmond, Washington: Microsoft Press, 2000. Review Chapter 6, "Tables."

Microsoft Corporation. *MCSE Training Kit: Microsoft SQL Server 2000 Database Design and Implementation*. Redmond, Washington: Microsoft Press, 2001. Read and complete the practices in Lesson 4 in Chapter 2, "Using Transact-SQL on a SQL Server Database," Lessons 1 and 3 in Chapter 4, "Implementing SQL Server Databases and Tables," Lessons 1 and 2 in Chapter 5, "Implementing Data Integrity," Lessons 1, 2, and 3 in Chapter 8, "Implementing Stored Procedures," Lessons 1, 2, and 3 in Chapter 9, "Implementing Triggers," Lessons 1, 2, and 3 in Chapter 10, "Implementing Views," and Lessons 1 and 2 in Chapter 11, "Implementing Indexes."

Objective 2.3

Microsoft SQL Server 2000 product documentation. To access Books Online, click the Start button, point to Programs, then Microsoft SQL Server, and then click Books Online. Click the Contents tab, double-click "Replication," and review "Partitioned Views."

Delaney, Kalen. *Inside Microsoft SQL Server 2000*. Redmond, Washington: Microsoft Press, 2000. Review Chapter 2, "A Tour of SQL Server: Data Replication."

Microsoft Corporation. *MCSE Training Kit: Microsoft SQL Server 2000 Database Design and Implementation*. Redmond, Washington: Microsoft Press, 2001. Read and complete the practices in Lesson 2, Chapter 14, "Maintaining and Optimizing SQL Server Database."

Objective 2.4

Microsoft SQL Server 2000 product documentation. To access Books Online, click the Start button, point to Programs, then Microsoft SQL Server, and then click Books Online. Click the Contents tab and review "Transact-SQL Reference" and "Troubleshooting."

Microsoft SQL Server 2000 product documentation. To access Books Online, click the Start button, point to Programs, then Microsoft SQL Server, and then click Books Online. Click the Contents tab and double-click the "Optimizing Database Performance" topic. Then review "Physical Database Design" under "Database Design."

Microsoft SQL Server 2000 product documentation. To access Books Online, click the Start button, point to Programs, then Microsoft SQL Server, and then click Books Online. Click the Contents tab and double-click the "Creating and Maintaining Databases" topic. Then review "Creating and Modifying a Table" under "Tables."

Microsoft Corporation. *MCSE Training Kit: Microsoft SQL Server 2000 Database Design and Implementation*. Redmond, Washington: Microsoft Press, 2001. Read and complete the practices in Lesson 2, Chapter 14, "Maintaining and Optimizing SQL Server Database."

OBJECTIVE 2.1

Create and alter databases.

The first step to creating databases is to plan how the databases will be created and distributed across the physical media. SQL Server 2000 provides so much flexibility in database creation and placement that a plan is required to properly design the physical implementation for optimal performance and flexibility.

Start by gathering information about your system. Accurate information might not be readily available as to how usage will occur, so be prepared to change your plan later to optimize performance.

Next, consider how you will partition the databases across the physical drives (if at all). Also, you should consider how many files or filegroups will need to be created and how the database should be placed on these filegroups.

It is critical to determine the optimal placement for the transaction log as well, and to try to ensure that there is no contention between the data being written and the transaction log being written.

Part of the database creation plan must also be the database maintenance plan. What recovery model will you use, and how do you plan to back up and restore databases, as well as perform necessary database console commands (DBCCs)? All of these questions need to be taken into consideration in determining how to design databases.

Objective 2.1 Questions

70-229.02.01.001

You are managing databases for a long distance phone company. One of these databases is used to temporarily hold millions of phone call records. After the billing processes are finished, you have to delete certain records from the tables, and you need to use your system disk resources conservatively. How would you create the database and what kind of settings would you use?

A. Create a small database and use the autogrow feature.

B. Create a large database and disable the autogrow feature.

C. Create a database, allow it to automatically grow, and enable the autoclose feature.

D. Create a database, allow it to automatically grow, and enable the autoshrink feature.

70-229.02.01.002

You have just expanded your server with a second high-speed RAID controller and disk drives. You want to take advantage of this new controller and drives. You have one primary database used by an application. How can you take advantage of the new expansion while disturbing operations as little as possible?

A. Back up the database and create one large logical drive spanning the two controllers.

B. Create a second database on the logical drive of the second controller and move some tables into the new database.

C. Add files to the filegroup of the database and transaction log and place them on the new controller's logical drive.

70-229.02.01.003

You are trying to design a system and optimize it for throughput. You have to decide how to organize your drives, tables, indexes, and so on. Your system contains two RAID controllers with three channels on each controller. Each channel has 40 MB/sec throughput. You cannot create logical drives spanning controllers, but you can create logical drives spanning channels on the same controller. Which of the following solutions would provide the best performance?

A. Create a logical disk spanning all three channels and place the system files, swap file, and the SQL Server executable files on this drive. Create the second logical drive spanning the three channels of the second controller, and place the transaction log and the database files on this drive.

B. Create a logical disk spanning all three channels and place the system files, swap file, the SQL Server executable files, and the transaction log on that logical disk. Create the second logical drive spanning the three channels of the second controller, and put the database files on the second logical drive.

C. Create a logical drive on the first controller's first channel only. Place the system and the page files on this logical drive. Create a second logical drive on the first controller's second and third channels. Place the database transaction log on the second logical drive. Create a third logical drive on the second controller spanning the three channels, and place the database and index files on the third logical drive.

D. Create a logical drive on the first controller's first channel only. Place the system and the page file on this logical drive. Create a second logical drive on the first controller's second and third channels. Create a third logical drive on the second controller spanning the three channels. When you create the database in the filegroup, you specify a file on the second logical drive and a file on the third logical drive for both the database and the transaction log.

70-229.02.01.004

You have deleted 10 million rows from the CallDetails table in MyDATA. Which statement would you use to make SQL Server resize the database file to its smallest possible size?

A. `ALTER DATABASE MyDATA SET RECOVERY SIMPLE`

B. `DBCC SHRINKDB`

C. `DBCC SHRINKFILE`

D. `DBCC SQLPERF SHRINKDB`

70-229.02.01.005

You have a server with a RAID controller with three channels, and each channel has 40 MB/sec throughput. Your system drive is created on a logical drive array using the first channel only. The data drive is created with the union of the second and third channel as a second logical drive. When you look at the disk performance, you realize that the data drive is overworked but the system drive has almost no activity. How would you reconfigure this system to have better performance?

A. Reconfigure the physical disk subsystem so that both the system and the data logical drives span all three channels.

B. Reconfigure the logical disk system, creating three logical drives with each one on its own channel. Place system, page file, and data on their own logical drives.

C. Reconfigure the system creating three logical drives with each one on its own channel. Place system, data, and transaction log on their own logical drive.

70-229.02.01.006

You have decided to create two filegroups for your database, a primary and a secondary. Which of the following are advantages to this approach? (Choose all that apply.)

A. The primary filegroup can be backed up separately from the secondary filegroup.

B. The filegroups can be checked for data consistency and integrity separately.

C. By separating the filegroups, both can contain historical data and be marked as read-only.

D. The primary filegroup can be small enough to contain only the system tables and placed on the most fault-tolerant drives, to help ensure point-of-failure recovery.

70-229.02.01.007

Which of the following RAID levels is best suited to the transaction log on a system using the full recovery model?

A. RAID 0

B. RAID 1

C. RAID 5

70-229.02.01.008

You have decided that you want to use raw partitions with your SQL Server database to improve performance. Does SQL Server support raw partitions, and how many data files can you place on a raw partition?

A. SQL Server no longer supports raw partitions.

B. SQL Server supports raw partitions, and the maximum file number is unlimited.

C. SQL Server supports raw partitions, and the maximum file number is one.

Objective 2.1 Answers

70-229.02.01.001

▶ Correct Answers: D

A. **Incorrect:** Creating a small database and enabling the autogrow feature will conserve space. However, when the database grows after the processing is done, the database will retain its largest size. You have to enable the autoshrink feature to allow SQL Server to shrink the database.

B. **Incorrect:** Creating a large database improves performance because the database does not have to allocate data while it processes new records. In this case, after you delete the unnecessary records, the database will retain its size. You need to shrink the database as soon as possible to conserve disk space. Having a fixed size database might interrupt your operation if the incoming data is more than the database is able to hold.

C. **Incorrect:** Although creating a database and letting it automatically grow is correct, enabling autoclose will not help to conserve disk space. Autoclose enables SQL Server to shut the database down when all resources are freed and all users are disconnected. You have to enable autoshrink to conserve disk space.

D. **Correct:** Databases are created by default with autogrow enabled. This feature allows the database to grow when it requires more space to hold the data, indexes, and other database-related information. Enabling autoshrink causes the database to resize itself when data is removed from the database. SQL Server 2000 will periodically check the database and will shrink the database files when possible. Be aware that there is a performance hit when the database is growing.

70-229.02.01.002

▶ Correct Answers: C

A. **Incorrect:** You could create one logical drive spanning the two controllers if the controllers allow it. It would create a relatively big interruption because you need to back up the database and then create the logical drive, format it, re-create the database, and restore the database. You should add new files to the filegroup of the database and the transaction log and place them on the new logical drive.

B. **Incorrect:** If you wouldn't break referential integrity, you can do this, but the application might have to be changed. You could horizontally partition the data, but you will have to move data from one database to the other periodically. You should add new files to the filegroup of the database and the transaction log and place them on the new logical drive.

C. **Correct:** If you expand the database this way, you will not interrupt the operation of the database at all. SQL Server will automatically start using the files on the second logical disk as soon as it requires more pages for new data.

70-229.02.01.003

► Correct Answers: D

A. **Incorrect:** In this case you will have both logical drives with the maximum of 120 MB/sec throughput. This is overkill for the system, page, and SQL Server executables. These files are accessed infrequently, whereas the database is limited to only 120 MB/sec throughput without utilizing the available system resources.

B. **Incorrect:** In this scenario you are utilizing the controllers more evenly, but you are still limiting the possible performance. Moving the transaction log to another controller improves the performance for insert, update, and delete, but it's not utilizing the resources for data retrieval.

C. **Incorrect:** In this case you are using the controller more evenly, but you still do not have the best configuration. The system files are fine on a single channel because they are accessed less frequently. The transaction log is limited to only 80 MB/sec, which can slow insert, update, and delete transactions. The database files are limited to only 120 MB/sec throughput.

D. **Correct:** This is the best configuration of the given examples. The system files are on their own logical drive and have plenty of throughput of 40 MB/sec. These files are accessed less frequently. Creating both the database and transaction log spanning two logical drives produces the maximum throughput of 200 MB/sec.

70-229.02.01.004

► Correct Answers: C

A. **Incorrect:** The SET RECOVERY option allows the recovery model to be set, and SIMPLE is the nonlogged option, but this will not affect any actions that were taken previously. With ALTER DATABASE you can add or remove files from the database, but before that you have to execute DBCC SHRINKFILE with the EMPTYFILE argument. You have to use DBCC SHRINKFILE to force the database to shrink the given file. You cannot make the database smaller than the model database.

B. **Incorrect:** DBCC SHRINKDB is not supported in Microsoft SQL Server 7 or SQL Server 2000. You have to shrink the data files of the database individually. You have to use DBCC SHRINKFILE to force the database to shrink one of its files. Database size will never be smaller than the model database.

C. **Correct:** DBCC SHRINKFILE is used to instruct SQL Server to try to shrink its file to a smaller size. It can be used on files in a database or in the transaction log. Database size will never be smaller than the model database.

D. **Incorrect:** DBCC SQLPERF does not have a SHRINKDB option. DBCC SQLPERF provides statistics about the use transaction log space in all databases. DBCC SHRINKFILE is used to instruct SQL Server to try to shrink its file to a smaller size. It can be used on the files in a database or in the transaction log. Database size will never be smaller than the model database.

70-229.02.01.005

► Correct Answers: A

A. **Correct:** In this case all logical drives will span all three channels, so the data drive will have more throughput. For example: If the channels are 40 MB/sec, you will have 120 MB/sec throughput compared to the original 80 MB/sec.

B. **Incorrect:** Configuring a RAID system this way will decrease database performance. The system did not have any problem while the system files and page file were on the same controller. So separating them and giving each its own channel will not improve the system performance. Instead, this configuration will to some degree degrade performance. In the original configuration, the data drive had 80 MB/sec throughput, but in this configuration it has only 40 MB/sec.

C. **Incorrect:** Although in some circumstances it is a good idea to separate the data and the log files onto different drives, in this case it will not improve the performance. You are still limited to the maximum 80 MB/sec throughput for the database, and this configuration will not take advantage of the remaining 40 MB/sec.

70-229.02.01.006

▸ Correct Answers: A, B, and D

A. **Correct:** Because there is no need to back up data that has not changed, seldom-changed data can be put on the secondary filegroup. You could then choose to back up the primary filegroup only, to ensure that the system databases are always intact. This approach allows a partial restore. Filegroups provide much more flexibility for performance and maintenance.

B. **Correct:** Filegroups can have DBCC CHECKFILEGROUP run on each separate filegroup. This approach can be advantageous when a system's maintenance window is too small for both filegroups to have DBCCs performed, or when data changes little on the secondary filegroup. Filegroups provide much more flexibility for performance and maintenance.

C. **Incorrect:** The primary filegroup can never be marked as read-only. However, by creating two or more filegroups, the secondary filegroup data can be read-only, whereas the data in the primary filegroup would be read-write.

D. **Correct:** To have point-of-failure recovery, the primary filegroup must be intact. If you make it small and protected from the rest of the data, this filegroup has a better chance of remaining intact.

70-229.02.01.007

▸ Correct Answers: B

A. **Incorrect:** RAID 0 is not recommended for any SQL Server files without any other availability plan because RAID 0 provides no redundancy. Because the transaction log is required for full recovery, there must be some kind of redundancy in the system.

B. **Correct:** RAID 1 is excellent for the transaction log. It provides mirroring for redundancy and is optimal for sequential writes because there is no striping involved in this level. Because the transaction log is a sequential wrap-around write, this level is both fault-tolerant and high-performing for the transaction log.

C. **Incorrect:** RAID 5 uses parity, as well as striping, to provide fault tolerance without the expense of duplicate drives used for mirroring, placing some data on all discs. This is excellent for read operations, because it uses fewer discs than RAID 1, but it is not optimal for the transaction log, which will perform mostly sequential writes.

70-229.02.01.008

▶ Correct Answers: C

A. **Incorrect:** SQL Server supports raw partitions and FAT and NTFS also. Although raw partitions can yield some performance improvement, they can also make SQL Server management more complex.

B. **Incorrect:** Although SQL Server supports raw partitions, the maximum file number per partition is one. A raw partition does not have a file system, so the whole partition is treated as a single file.

C. **Correct:** SQL Server supports raw partitions with a single file per partition. For each file you have to create a partition. Some of the built-in features, such as autogrow, are not available with raw partitions. You have to use just a drive letter assigned to the raw partition or a mounting point.

OBJECTIVE 2.2

Create and alter database objects.

After the databases have been created, the database objects must be created, including tables and views. Creating database objects also requires a physical implementation plan. You should already have a logical model that will guide you for the creation of the tables as far as the names, columns, data types, and constraints. However, now is the time to optimize each of these parts of the object creation for the physical implementation.

Determine how you will use **views** in your system. Some shops use views only for database access, leaving the underlying tables unavailable to developer access. This approach can be complex to work with but is quite flexible because it allows changes to be made to the underlying table objects without changing any of the code that is used against the system. In SQL Server, indexed views can now be used to help with specific performance problems that might be occurring with certain queries.

You will need a plan as to where to place the database objects within the files and filegroups. This allows you to tune your system's performance by controlling how and where data is stored physically. Separating often-used tables on separate filegroups can enhance performance by providing parallel read and write access if they are on different drives.

Again, SQL Server 2000 provides a great deal of flexibility and control over database object creation and placement for performance, as well as the ease with which objects can be modified or altered.

Objective 2.2 Questions

70-229.02.02.001

You use this syntax to create a table:

```
CREATE TABLE Customers (
CustomerID    int         IDENTITY (1,10),
LastName      varchar(25)    NOT NULL,
FirstName     varchar(25)    NOT NULL,
MiddleName    varchar(1),
Add1          varchar(20),
City          varchar(20),
State         varchar(2),
ZipCode       varchar(5)
)
```

Which results will this produce? (Choose all answers that apply.)

A. The IDENTITY value starts at 10 and gets incremented with a value of 1.

B. The IDENTITY value gets generated automatically, and this column can be updated.

C. The IDENTITY value gets generated automatically, and this column cannot be updated.

D. None of the columns can have a NULL value.

70-229.02.02.002

You use the following statement to create a table:

```
CREATE TABLE Logging (
LogID         uniqueidentifier    DEFAULT ( NEWID ()),
Title         varchar (25)        NOT NULL,
Data          text,
Status        int                 NOT NULL
)
```

Which results will this produce? (Choose all that apply.)

A. LogID, Title, and Status cannot be NULL.

B. LogID will have a default value of a new GUID and can be updated.

C. LogID and Data are nullable, whereas Title and Status must have a value other than NULL.

D. TEXT is limited to 4000 characters if no size is defined.

70-229.02.02.003

You use the following statement to create a table:

```
CREATE TABLE Orders (
OrderID       uniqueidentifier    NOT NULL DEFAULT( NEWID() )
CONSTRAINT pk_Orders PRIMARY KEY,
CustomerID    long                NOT NULL,
Date          datetime
)
```

Which results will this produce? (Choose all that apply.)

A. The uniqueidentifier data type will generate unique integer numbers.

B. OrderID value will be a GUID, and it will be used as the PRIMARY KEY of this table.

C. Defines OrderID, CustomerID, and Date values.

70-229.02.02.004

You are planning to create an index for a large table with two columns used to identify rows. Users need to access data quickly in sorted order, and duplicates are permitted. Which indexing strategy should you choose?

A. Unique, composite, and clustered

B. Nonunique, composite, and nonclustered

C. Nonunique, composite, and clustered

D. Nonclustered

70-229.02.02.005

You need to change your Orders table by adding a new column. This column must be of integer type, cannot have a null value, and can accept the following numbers: 1, 3, 5, 7, and 9. A default value of 1 should be assigned. Which of the following is true?

A. You can achieve the requirement by executing the following Transact-SQL statement: `ALTER TABLE Orders ADD (SpecialValue  int not null check (SpecialValue in (1,3,5,7,9))`

B. You can achieve the requirement by executing the following Transact-SQL statement: `ALTER TABLE Orders ADD (  SpecialValue int  not null  default (1) check (SpecialValue in (1,3,5,7,9))`

C. Columns with a not null value cannot be added to a table.

D. You cannot add a column and a constraint in one statement.

70-229.02.02.006

You have created a view with the option of SCHEMABINDING. What effect will this have on the view?

A. Prior to execution of the view, the schema will be checked for changes to the underlying tables and views.

B. SQL Server will return information about the view instead of the underlying tables and views when browse-mode metadata is requested.

C. SCHEMABINDING binds the view to the schema, so the SELECT statement must include the two-part names of tables, views, or user-defined functions referenced.

70-229.02.02.007

You have two tables with the same schema definition. One table will store East Coast data, and the other will store the data for the West Coast. You want to create a view that returns all the rows from both tables. You write the following statement:

```
CREATE VIEW AllData as
SELECT * FROM EastCoast
UNION ALL
SELECT * FROM WestCoast
```

What is the difference between UNION and UNION ALL?

A. There is no difference between UNION and UNION ALL.

B. UNION ALL is not supported in SQL Server 2000.

C. UNION returns everything from the first table and everything that does not already exist from the second table. UNION ALL returns everything from both tables.

D. UNION returns only unique records from both tables. UNION ALL returns all records from both tables.

70-229.02.02.008

Where does SQL Server keep the scripts for views, and what happens if you use the ENCRYPTION option?

A. View scripts are kept in the syscomments system table, and using ENCRYPTION stores the script coded and the view cannot be replicated. If you use the ENCRYPTION option, you should save the script.

B. View scripts are kept in the sysviews system table, and using ENCRYPTION will garble the text output if you try to view the script. It has no effect on replication.

C. View scripts are kept in the sysviews system table, and ENCRYPTION will cause the script not to be stored in SQL Server—only the execution plan will be stored. The view cannot be replicated.

D. View scripts are kept in the sysviewdetails system table; using ENCRYPTION will store the script coded and the view can be replicated.

70-229.02.02.009

You have a stored procedure in your SQL Server database to calculate bonuses for employees. The logic for this procedure is very complex, and you do not want anyone to see the logic in your database even if they have administrative rights. What option is correct to use with your CREATE PROCEDURE statement?

A. `WITH SECURITY ON`

B. `WITH ENCRYPTION PASSWORD 'password'`

C. `WITH ENCRYPTION`

70-229.02.02.010

You have a stored procedure in your SQL Server database using atypical and temporary values. You do not want SQL Server to cache the execution plan for this stored procedure. What is the attribute you should use when creating the stored procedure?

A. WITH NOCACHE

B. WITH RECOMPILE

C. WITH NEW PLAN

70-229.02.02.011

After analyzing the performance of your SQL Server database, you find out that one of your tables is causing SQL Server to provide slow performance. To be precise, you find out that the indexes on a table are not effective. You come to the conclusion that your primary key should not be clustered, whereas a second index should be. Which of the following statements is correct?

A. You can re-create your primary key to use nonclustered indexes and your secondary index to use clustered indexes.

B. You cannot achieve the requirement because a primary key is always created as a clustered index.

C. You can create your primary key nonclustered as long as no other table references it with a foreign key constraint.

70-229.02.02.012

You have a table and you need to create an index on one of the columns. This column has duplicate values. You know that no more duplicate values will be entered into the table, but the existing duplicate values must be kept in the table. You do not want to allow any more duplicate keys entered into the table. Which of the following statements is true?

A. You cannot achieve the requirement. You have to remove the duplicates and then create an index with the UNIQUE option.

B. You can achieve the requirement when creating the index by using the UNIQUE and IGNORE_DUP_KEY options.

C. You can achieve the requirements using the IGNORE_DUP_KEY option.

70-229.02.02.013

You have Table1 with static data, whereas Table2 is volatile. What FILLFACTOR would you use on indexes created for both tables?

A. Low FILLFACTOR for Table1 and high FILLFACTOR for Table2

B. High FILLFACTOR for Table1 and low FILLFACTOR for Table2

C. High FILLFACTOR for both tables

Objective 2.2 Answers

70-229.02.02.001

► Correct Answers: C

A. **Incorrect:** An IDENTITY column takes the following parameters: the first is the seed value, and the second is the increment value. This example creates a Customer table; CustomerID will be generated as soon as a new record is inserted into the table. LastName and FirstName are mandatory, whereas the rest of the columns are optional.

B. **Incorrect:** Although the first part of the answer was correct, the second part is incorrect. IDENTITY columns cannot be updated.

C. **Correct:** This example creates a Customer table; CustomerID will be generated as soon as a new record is inserted into the table. An IDENTITY column is not updateable. LastName and FirstName are mandatory, whereas the rest of the columns are optional.

D. **Incorrect:** If neither NULL nor NOT NULL is defined and the data type is not an IDENTITY column, the column will be nullable. LastName and FirstName are not nullable, whereas the rest can have a NULL value.

70-229.02.02.002

► Correct Answers: B and C

A. **Incorrect:** LogID is not defined as not nullable. If you do not want to accept NULLs in this column, you should declare it as **LogID uniqueidentifier NOT NULL DEFAULT(NEWID** ()). This example creates a table, LogID, and Data can accept NULL, whereas Title and Status must have a value other than NULL. LogID will be populated with a new globally unique identifier (GUID), and this column can be updated.

B. **Correct:** LogID will have a new GUID as a value as soon as a new record is inserted into the table. This column can be updated or nulled. This example creates a table, LogID, and Data can accept NULL, whereas Title and Status must have a value other than NULL.

C. **Correct:** Uniqueidentifier is just another data type. It does not create a value as IDENTITY does, and IDENTITY exclusively sets the column to not updateable. This example creates a table, and LogID and Data can accept NULL, whereas Title and Status must have a value other than NULL.

D. **Incorrect:** TEXT is a data type, and its size cannot be defined as it can be with NUMERIC or VARCHAR. TEXT is capable of storing up to 231 – 1 (2,147,483,647) bytes. TEXT is used for non-Unicode strings, whereas NTEXT is used for Unicode strings.

70-229.02.02.003

► Correct Answers: B and C

A. **Incorrect:** A uniqueidentifier column can accept only a valid GUID. In this example OrderID will have a value of a GUID, and this column will be used as the PRIMARY KEY column. CustomerID cannot have a value of NULL, whereas Date does not have to have a value.

B. **Correct:** OrderID cannot have a value of NULL because of the NOT NULL clause; by default it will have a new GUID and be the PRIMARY KEY of this table.

C. **Correct:** CREATE TABLE defines all the columns of a table. The column definitions of the table must include the name and type of the columns. The data type must be either a system-defined data type or a user-defined data type. In addition, you can constrain each column as a NULL or NOT NULL. You can also define default values, PRIMARY KEY constraint, and FOREIGN KEY constraints or CHECK constraints.

70-229.02.02.004

► Correct Answers: C

A. **Incorrect:** Although composite and clustered are correct, unique is incorrect because this table must allow duplicates. A clustered index orders the data physically. You need a composite index because you have more than one column in the index. Duplicates are allowed, so a nonunique index is needed.

B. **Incorrect:** Although nonunique and composite are correct, nonclustered is incorrect. You should create a clustered index. A clustered index is ordered physically, which is useful when data is accessed in sorted order. Data in a nonclustered index is not sorted in the order of the index.

C. **Correct:** A clustered index orders the data physically. You need a composite index because you have more than one column in the index. Duplicates are allowed, so a nonunique index is needed.

D. **Incorrect:** You should create a clustered index. A clustered index is ordered physically, which is useful when data is accessed in sorted order. Data in a nonclustered index is not sorted in the order of the index. You should have chosen a nonunique, composite, clustered index.

70-229.02.02.005

► Correct Answers: B

A. **Incorrect:** If you add a column to a table with a not null option, you must use a default value. Not specifying the default value will cause an error. You need to insert the default between the not null and check.

B. **Correct:** Adding a column with a not null option and defining a default value produces the result you want. The CHECK constraint will be created correctly, and the name will be generated automatically. If naming the constraint is necessary, you have to add the constraint definition after a comma in the statement.

C. **Incorrect:** Columns with a not null value can be added to an existing table; however, a default value must be defined. If you try to add a column with the not null option but without a default value, SQL Server will generate an error. You can create the constraint two different ways within the same command, either by defining the constraint as an option of the column without a defined name or by specifying it after the column definition separated with a comma.

D. **Incorrect:** You can create the column definition and the constraint with the same statement. You can create the constraint two different ways within the same command, either by defining the constraint as an option of the column without a defined name or specifying it after the column definition separated with a comma.

70-229.02.02.006

► Correct Answers: C

A. **Incorrect:** The schema will not be checked every time the view is executed. If the underlying tables or views are changed and columns are removed from the tables or views, the execution might fail based on the changes at execution time. SCHEMABINDING will force binding of the schema to the view. You must include the two-part name, like object.name, for tables, views, or user-defined functions. Objects cannot be dropped while they are referenced from a view using SCHEMABINDING. In a view created with SCHEMABINDING, all columns are updateable except a column with a type of TIMESTAMP.

B. **Incorrect:** If you have to return browse-mode metadata, you need to use the VIEW_METADATA option. SCHEMABINDING will force binding of the schema to the view. You must include the two-part name, like object.name, for tables, views, or user-defined functions. Objects cannot be dropped while they are referenced from a view using SCHEMABINDING. In a view created with SCHEMABINDING, all columns are updateable except a column with a type of TIMESTAMP.

C. **Correct:** SCHEMABINDING will force binding of the schema to the view. You must include the two-part name, like object.name, for tables, views, or user-defined functions. Objects cannot be dropped while they are referenced from a view using SCHEMABINDING. In a view created with SCHEMABINDING, all columns are updateable except a column with a type of TIMESTAMP.

70-229.02.02.007

▶ Correct Answers: D

A. **Incorrect:** UNION and UNION ALL are not the same commands. The UNION operator returns two or more SELECT statement results in a single result set. These result sets must have the same number of columns and compatible data types. By default UNION will remove duplicates from the result set; if you use UNION ALL, all records will be returned in the result set.

B. **Incorrect:** UNION ALL is a valid option statement in SQL Server 2000. The UNION operator returns two or more SELECT statement results in a single result set. These result sets must have the same number of columns and compatible data types. By default UNION will remove duplicates from the result set; if you use UNION ALL, all records will be returned in the result set.

C. **Incorrect:** This answer is incorrect because duplicate records from the first table will also be removed. The UNION operator returns two or more SELECT statement results in a single result set. These result sets must have the same number of columns and compatible data types. By default UNION will remove duplicates from the result set; if you use UNION ALL, all records will be returned in the result set.

D. **Correct:** The UNION operator returns two or more SELECT statement results in a single result set. These result sets must have the same number of columns and compatible data types. By default UNION will remove duplicates from the result set; if you use UNION ALL, all records will be returned in the result set.

70-229.02.02.008

► Correct Answers: A

A. **Correct:** View scripts are kept in the syscomments system table. Using ENCRYPTION will code the script so that it cannot be viewed and causes the view not to be replicated.

B. **Incorrect:** View scripts are kept in the syscomments system table instead of the sysviews system table. A sysviews system table does not exist in SQL Server 2000. View scripts are kept in the syscomments system table; using ENCRYPTION will store the script coded and the view cannot be replicated. If you use the ENCRYPTION option, you should save the script.

C. **Incorrect:** View scripts are kept in the syscomments system table; using ENCRYPTION will store the script coded and the view cannot be replicated. If you use the ENCRYPTION option, you should save the script.

D. **Incorrect:** View scripts are kept in the syscomments system table; using ENCRYPTION will store the script coded and the view cannot be replicated. If you use the ENCRYPTION option, you should save the script.

70-229.02.02.009

► Correct Answers: C

A. **Incorrect:** To disable the viewing of the stored procedure code, you have to use the WITH ENCRYPTION option when you create the stored procedure. After you encrypt a stored procedure, there is no way to decrypt it.

B. **Incorrect:** Although the correct attribute to encrypt a stored procedure is WITH ENCRYPTION, you cannot specify a password. After a stored procedure is encrypted, there is no way to decrypt it in SQL Server.

C. **Correct:** The WITH ENCRYPTION option on the CREATE PROCEDURE statement will force SQL Server to encrypt the Transact-SQL code within the stored procedure. After the code is encrypted, it is no longer viewable.

70-229.02.02.010

► Correct Answers: B

A. **Incorrect:** To force SQL Server to recompile and not cache the execution plan, you need to use the WITH RECOMPILE attribute when creating the stored procedure.

B. **Correct:** The WITH RECOMPILE option will force SQL Server not to cache the execution plan for the stored procedure and to recompile it each time it executes.

C. **Incorrect:** WITH NEW PLAN is not supported in SQL Server. To force SQL Server not to cache the execution plan, you need to use the WITH RECOMPILE option when creating the stored procedure.

70-229.02.02.011

► Correct Answers: A

A. **Correct:** A primary key can be created with a nonclustered index. By default SQL Server uses clustered indexes, but this can be changed when creating the table or after the table has been created.

B. **Incorrect:** A common misunderstanding is to assume that a primary key can only be a clustered index. This is the default that SQL Server provides, and most commonly it is the correct indexing for primary keys. However, it can be changed either at table creation or with the ALTER TABLE statement after the table has been created.

C. **Incorrect:** Although the first part of the answer is correct—a primary key can be created using a nonclustered index—the second part is incorrect. For foreign keys it does not matter what kind of index is used on the referenced column, if any.

70-229.02.02.012

▸ Correct Answers: B

A. **Incorrect:** You can achieve the requirements using the UNIQUE and IGNORE_DUP_KEY options when creating the index. UNIQUE will force every insert and update to have a unique value, whereas IGNORE_DUP_KEY allows SQL Server not to check the existing data in the table.

B. **Correct:** Using the UNIQUE option will force SQL Server to check every update and insert against the existing data ensuring that no duplicates will be entered into the table. IGNORE_DUP_KEY allows SQL Server not to check the existing data in the table when the index is created.

C. **Incorrect:** Although IGNORE_DUP_KEY allows SQL Server not to check the existing data for duplication, it does not protect against updates and inserts entering duplicate values. You have to also use the UNIQUE option. UNIQUE will force all updates and inserts to be checked against the existing data and will not allow duplicates.

70-229.02.02.013

▸ Correct Answers: B

A. **Incorrect:** For tables with static data, you should use high FILLFACTOR so SQL Server will place more data on index pages. For volatile tables you should set a low FILLFACTOR, allowing new data to be inserted into the index pages and preventing page splits.

B. **Correct:** High FILLFACTOR allows SQL Server to place more data on index pages, whereas low FILLFACTOR leaves more room on index pages. These settings prevent SQL Server from splitting pages as frequently, which improves the performance.

C. **Incorrect:** Although high FILLFACTOR is good for static tables, it is not optimal for volatile tables. Volatile tables need space on index pages; if less space is available on the index pages, SQL Server will be forced to split the pages, which decreases performance.

OBJECTIVE 2.3

Alter database objects to support replication and partitioned views.

SQL Server 2000 allows you to replicate, copy, and modify data across SQL Server servers in your enterprise. SQL Server 2000 supports **snapshot**, **transactional**, and **merge replication**. SQL Server 2000 also includes several methods and options for replication design, monitoring, and administration that are needed for distributing data while keeping data consistent. SQL replication has many benefits, such as allowing different sites to keep a copy of the same data, allowing separate **online transaction processing (OLTP)** and **online analytical processing (OLAP)** databases, allowing users to work in disconnected environments with changes propagated when reconnected, increasing aggregate read performance, and providing support for standby databases. You should think about SQL Server replication when you have to solve one of the following problems: copy or replicate data to one or more sites, distribute data on a scheduled basis, distribute changes to other databases, allow multiple sites to change the data and then merge the changes, or use databases in an online/offline environment.

Snapshot replication distributes data as it appeared at the moment when the snapshot was taken. It does not monitor changes made between the replications; rather, it copies the whole data. Snapshot replication is best for infrequently replicated data where latency is not a problem. Snapshot replication is helpful when data is mostly static and does not change often, when it is acceptable if the data is out of date, or when replicating small amounts of data.

Transactional replication uses snapshots the first time to push the data to the subscribers, and then when changes are made at the publisher, the changes get captured and sent to the subscribers. Transactional replication is helpful when you want changes to be propagated to the subscribers as they occur, when you need transactions to support the **ACID** (**atomicity**, **consistency**, **isolation**, and **durability**) properties, and when subscribers are reliably connected to the publisher. In transactional replication, only the publisher data is changed—the subscribers should be read-only.

Merge replication works like transactional replication, but both the publisher and the subscriber can change the data. Changes will be merged together at the publisher. Merge replication allows sites to work autonomously and, at a later time, merge the updates into a single database at the publisher. After the changes are rolled up, the changes will be pushed to all subscribers. Merge replication is useful when multiple subscribers need to modify the data, when subscribers need to receive data and make changes offline and later synchronize the changes, and when you do not expect any conflicts when data is updated at multiple sites.

Objective 2.3 Questions

70-229.02.03.001

You are working for an e-commerce company. You want to ease the load on SQL Server, and you decide to add additional servers for read-only operations. The Products list is changed quite infrequently and should be rolled out as a single transaction. What kind of SQL Server replication would you use?

A. Transactional replication

B. Snapshot replication

C. Merge replication

70-229.02.03.002

You are working for a roadside service company. Data centers are located all over the country and changes are made only to the corporate database, but customer information is read on all locations. Changes to the database must be replicated as soon as possible to the subscriber servers. What kind of replication would you use?

A. Transactional replication

B. Snapshot replication

C. Merge replication

70-229.02.03.003

You are developing a database design and implementation for a sales system. The requirement is that a subset of the database will be downloaded into the salesperson's laptop and will be changed there. When the salesperson reconnects, his or her changes must be merged into the corporate database. What kind of replication would you use?

A. Transactional replication

B. Snapshot replication

C. Merge replication

70-229.02.03.004

You are scaling out your database and you add a second server. On both servers you have a table called Orders. You create a partitioned view called vOrders. RegionID is the column you have used to partition the data on, and it is part of the primary key. What do you have to do with the tables to set up partitioning correctly?

A. Create indexes on both tables on the RegionID column.

B. Create a constraint on both tables to set the acceptable values for both tables.

C. Execute `sp_EnablePartitioning on (Server1.MyDB.Orders, Server2.MyDB.Orders).`

D. You have to create a partitioned index on the vOrders view as follows: `CREATE NONCLUSTERED INDEX ndx_vOrders ON (RegionID) PARTITIONED ON Server1.MyDB.Orders values in (1 to 5), Server2.MyDB.Orders values in (6 to 10)`

70-229.02.03.005

What configuration do you have to set up on a database server to enable partitioning and get it to perform correctly?

A. Create remote servers in each server pointing to the other servers in the federated server cluster and enable lazy schema validation.

B. Create linked servers in each server pointing to other servers in the federated server cluster and enable lazy schema validation.

C. Create linked servers in each server pointing to other servers in the federated server cluster and disable lazy schema validation.

D. Create remote servers in each server pointing to the other servers in the federated server cluster and disable lazy schema validation.

70-229.02.03.006

You have a partitioned view. You want to create an index on this partitioned view so that you will have an indexed view. Which statement is correct?

A. You can create an indexed view on a partitioned view.

B. You cannot create an indexed view on a partitioned view.

C. You can create an indexed view on a partitioned view as long as the index is clustered.

70-229.02.03.007

You want to create indexed views. Which of the following SQL Server editions support indexed views? (Choose all that apply.)

A. SQL Server Developer Edition

B. SQL Server Standard Edition

C. SQL Server Enterprise Edition

Objective 2.3 Answers

70-229.02.03.001

► Correct Answers: B

A. **Incorrect:** Transactional replication is used to propagate changes to the subscribers as soon as they happen. Although this type of replication will do the job, it will introduce unnecessary processing on the publisher and the subscribers as well. You do not need to have the changes sent to the subscribers because they happen on an infrequent basis.

B. **Correct:** Snapshot replication is the correct answer because you do not need to have the changes as they happen. Transactional replication would introduce unnecessary processing on the servers. Merge replication would be also an incorrect answer because changes will only happen on the publisher server.

C. **Incorrect:** Merge replication is used when data can be changed either on the publisher or on the subscriber servers. In this case changes will be made only on the publisher server, and changes will be replicated on an infrequent basis. Both merge and transactional replication would introduce unnecessary processing and work on the servers.

70-229.02.03.002

► Correct Answers: A

A. **Correct:** Transactional replication is used to propagate changes to the subscribers as soon as they happen. Key features of the requirement are that changes are made only at the corporate office and changes must be replicated as soon as possible.

B. **Incorrect:** Snapshot replication is used when the data is changed very infrequently and data can be out of date while the updates happen on different servers. Key features of the requirement are that changes are made only at the corporate office and changes must be replicated as soon as possible. Only transactional replication can fulfill these requirements.

C. **Incorrect:** Merge replication is used when data can be changed on either the publisher or the subscriber servers. In this case data can be changed only at the corporate office, and changes must be replicated as soon as possible. Although merge replication would work correctly, the merge aspect of this replication would introduce unwanted overhead on the servers, which was not part of the requirement.

70-229.02.03.003

▶ Correct Answers: C

A. **Incorrect:** Transactional replication only allows data to be changed at the publisher. In this case data will be changed both at the publisher and at the subscribers. Based on the requirements, merge replication should be implemented. Merge replication allows data to be changed both at the publisher and at the subscribers.

B. **Incorrect:** Snapshot replication allows data to be changed at the publisher; also, snapshot replication is an expensive operation because the entire data set must be copied each time instead of just changes. Merge replication is the correct answer because merge replication allows data to be changed both at the publisher and at the subscribers.

C. **Correct:** Merge replication is the correct answer because it allows the data to be changed both at the publisher and at the subscribers. It will fulfill all the requirements in the scenario.

70-229.02.03.004

▶ Correct Answers: B

A. **Incorrect:** This is incorrect because it might speed up some of your queries, but you have to create a constraint on the RegionID and set the range for each partition. These constraints will be used by the query engine to determine which tables to access to satisfy your query. This will save valuable time for the server because it will not have to go across each and every machine for data.

B. **Correct:** You have to create a constraint on the RegionID columns in both databases on the Orders tables. The query engine will use these values to evaluate which servers it has to access to retrieve data to satisfy the query.

C. **Incorrect:** Sp_EnablePartitioning is not a valid SQL Server stored procedure. You have to create a constraint on the RegionID columns in both databases in the Orders tables. The query engine will use these values to evaluate which servers it has to access to retrieve data to satisfy the query.

D. **Incorrect:** This statement is incorrect. Although you can create an index on the view, it is not required. You have to create a constraint on the RegionID columns in both databases on the Orders tables. The query engine will use these values to evaluate which servers it has to access to retrieve data to satisfy the query.

70-229.02.03.005

► Correct Answers: B

A. **Incorrect:** Remote servers are used to enable stored procedure execution on a remote server. A client connected to one server can execute a stored procedure on a remote server without establishing a connection to the remote server. To enable partitioning, you have to set up linked servers and lazy schema validation using the sp_serveroption stored procedure. This optimizes performance by ensuring that the query processor does not request metadata for any of the linked tables until data is actually needed from the remote member table.

B. **Correct:** You have to create linked servers and use the sp_serveroption to enable lazy schema validation. This optimizes performance by ensuring that the query processor does not request metadata for any of the linked tables until data is actually needed from the remote member table.

C. **Incorrect:** The first part of the answer is correct, but the second is not. You need to have linked servers and enable lazy schema validation with the sp_serveroption stored procedure. Lazy schema validation optimizes performance by ensuring that the query processor does not request metadata for any of the linked tables until data is actually needed from the remote member table.

D. **Incorrect:** This answer is wrong in both ways; neither the server connection nor the lazy schema validation was presented correctly. Remote servers are used to enable stored procedure execution on a remote server. A client connected to one server can execute a stored procedure on a remote SQL Server without establishing a connection to the remote server. To enable partitioning, you have to set up linked servers and lazy schema validation using the sp_serveroption stored procedure. This optimizes performance by ensuring that the query processor does not request metadata for any of the linked tables until data is actually needed from the remote member table.

70-229.02.03.006

► Correct Answers: B

A. **Incorrect:** To create an indexed view, all referenced tables must be in the same database. This exclusivity prohibits a partitioned view. You can improve performance by creating indexes on each table used by the partitioned view.

B. **Correct:** You cannot use indexed and partitioned views together. Indexed views require that the tables reside in the same database.

C. **Incorrect:** Indexed views and partitioned views are mutually exclusive. Indexed views require the underlying tables to reside in the same database, whereas partitioned views are scattered across multiple instances of SQL Server.

70-229.02.03.007

▶ Correct Answers: A and C

A. **Correct:** SQL Server Developer Edition and SQL Server Enterprise Edition are the only editions that support indexed views.

B. **Incorrect:** SQL Server Standard Edition does not support indexed views.

C. **Correct:** SQL Server Developer Edition and SQL Server Enterprise Edition are the only editions that support indexed views.

OBJECTIVE 2.4

Troubleshoot failed object creation.

The first step in troubleshooting failed object creation is to check the syntax of your Transact-SQL statement. If the syntax is correct, check the relationships of the SQL Server objects involved in the operation. Usually the problem lies either in the object relationship or in not providing enough information for SQL Server to fulfill your request.

Dropping an object is most commonly interrupted because of the relationship with other objects such as foreign keys or constraints such as NOT NULL.

Modifying a column can be interrupted because the change would cause data corruption or truncation. Expanding a table with new columns could be interrupted because you did not supply enough information even though the syntax is correct. A good example of this is adding a new column to a table with the NOT NULL attribute but without including a default value.

Troubleshooting failed object creation is much more difficult than creating new objects. You have to look at existing objects and their interactions with changes and new objects.

Objective 2.4 Questions

70-229.02.04.001

You have an existing Customers table with customers' information. You need to add a column called Privileged with a data type of int. This column cannot have the value of NULL. You execute the following Transact-SQL statement and receive the following error code. How can you modify your statement to execute successfully and achieve the desired result?

```
ALTER TABLE Customers ADD Test INT NOT NULL
ERROR CODE:
Server: Msg 4901, Level 16, State 1, Line 1
ALTER TABLE only allows columns to be added that can contain nulls or have a DEFAULT
definition specified. Column 'test' cannot be added to table 'customers' because it
does not allow nulls and does not specify a DEFAULT definition.
```

A. You cannot modify the statement to achieve the required result without removing all the data from the table, making the changes, and then repopulating the table. If a default is defined, SQL Server will be able to update all existing records to this value, so it will not have to break the NOT NULL constraint.

B. You cannot modify the statement because you cannot add a NOT NULL column to a table.

C. You have to modify the statement as follows: `ALTER TABLE Customers ADD Test INT NOT NULL WITH FORCE`.

D. You have to define a default value.

70-229.02.04.002

You have modified your Customer table with the following Transact-SQL statement: `ALTER TABLE Customers ADD Privileged INT NOT NULL DEFAULT (0)`. The business requirements have changed and you no longer need the Privileged column. You execute the following statement and receive the following error message. How can you resolve the problem?

```
ALTER TABLE DROP COLUMN Privileged
Server: Msg 5074, Level 16, State 1, Line 1
The object 'DF__customers__privileged__5441852A' is dependent on column 'privileged'.
Server: Msg 4922, Level 16, State 1, Line 1
```

A. You have to drop the foreign key constraint referencing the Privileged column before you can drop the column itself.

B. You have to drop the default value (DF) before you can drop the column itself.

C. You have to drop the constraint (NOT NULL) before you can drop the column itself.

70-229.02.04.003

You created a view on a table called Testing123 with the following code: `CREATE VIEW vTesting123 AS SELECT * FROM Testing123`. After a few days you receive e-mails from the users with the following error message:

```
Server: Msg 208, Level 16, State 1, Procedure vTesting123, Line 1
Invalid object name 'Testing123'.
Server: Msg 4413, Level 16, State 1, Line 1
Could not use view or function 'vTesting123' because of binding errors.
```

What could cause this error?

A. Someone has modified the Testing123 table and did not rebind it with the view. The view still has the previous compilation and could not bind to the table.

B. Testing123 has been removed or renamed from the database, and the view cannot bind to it because it no longer exists.

C. Access rights have been changed, and users have no longer have access to the Testing123 table, only to the vTesting123 view.

Objective 2.4 Answers

70-229.02.04.001

► Correct Answers: D

A. **Incorrect:** Although this response would work, it does not achieve the requested modification. SQL Server allows you to add a column with a NOT NULL column as long as you also provide a default value.

B. **Incorrect:** A table can be modified with a column of NOT NULL constraint if a default is also provided. If a default is defined, SQL Server will be able to update all existing records to this value so it will not have to break the NOT NULL constraint.

C. **Incorrect:** SQL Server does not have an option to force an alteration on a table. You should define a default value. If a default is defined, SQL Server will be able to update all existing records to this value so it will not have to break the NOT NULL constraint.

D. **Correct:** If you define a default value, SQL Server will be able to add the new column to the table. SQL Server will use this value and update all existing records. This value will also be used when new records are inserted into the table and no value has been defined for the new record.

70-229.02.04.002

► Correct Answers: C

A. **Incorrect:** The error message does not imply a foreign key constraint referencing the Privileged column. It shows that a constraint is defined on the column. This constraint was created by the usage of the NOT NULL attribute when the column was created. The constraint must be removed before the column can be dropped.

B. **Incorrect:** This error message shows that a constraint is on the column. Defining a column with a default value does not create a constraint on the column. In the example code, we used the NOT NULL and it will create a constraint on the column. You have to drop the constraint before you can drop the column.

C. **Correct:** SQL Server reminded you that you still have a dependency issue before you can remove the column. The NOT NULL clause caused SQL Server to place a constraint on the column when it was created. Dropping the constraint will allow you to drop the column from the table.

70-229.02.04.003

▶ Correct Answers: B

A. **Incorrect:** SQL Server does not keep binding information between objects; therefore, every time the view is compiled or accessed, dependencies will be checked.

B. **Correct:** Someone has removed or renamed the Testing123 table. As a result, when the view is executed, SQL Server cannot find the table and the execution fails.

C. **Incorrect:** First, the error message would reflect permission violation and not invalid object names. Second, if the users have access privileges to access vTesting123, they do not need additional access rights for the Testing123 table.

OBJECTIVE DOMAIN 3

Retrieving and Modifying Data

The Retrieving and Modifying Data objective domain deals with building and executing Transact-SQL statements and processing **result sets**. Result sets can be retrieved either in a tabular (or relational) result set or in **eXtensible Markup Language (XML)** format.

Microsoft SQL Server applications connect to a database using one of the following two methods:

- Applications can use database **application programming interfaces (APIs)** such as **ADO**, **OLE DB**, or **ODBC**. With these access methods, SQL Server returns results in a tabular result set.

  Internet applications can use ADO or **Uniform Resource Locators (URLs)** to execute **XPath** queries on the computer running SQL Server. (XPath is a language used to access an XML document.)

- Data also can be manipulated by using the **bulk copy program (BCP)** or **Data Transformation Services (DTS)**.

  The BCP utility is used to export and import data between servers and data files and provides excellent performance. The BCP utility also allows the database operator to specify file formats.

DTS provides great flexibility to export and import data from different file formats and providers. You can export and import data from an ODBC or OLE DB data source and manipulate the data. These jobs can be saved in different packages and reused repeatedly. DTS provides a rich interface for application developers to interface with SQL Server.

Heterogeneous data can be manipulated, including other ODBC data sources and XML documents.

SQL Server 2000 also introduces new XML support, including the FOR XML clause for SELECT statements, which returns result sets in a number of different XML formats.

Tested Skills and Suggested Practices

The skills that you need to successfully master the Retrieving and Modifying Data objective domain on the *Designing and Implementing Databases with Microsoft SQL Server 2000 Enterprise Edition* exam include:

- **Using DTS and BCP.**
  - Practice 1: Use BCP to export data from a database to a file in text format and load the data into another table.
  - Practice 2: Load data into a table containing data and indexes. Examine the performance when no indexes exist on the table compared to the performance when indexes already exist.
  - Practice 3: Use DTS to load data in a comma-delimited format into a SQL Server database.
  - Practice 4: Use DTS to export data using a Transact-SQL SELECT statement, performing a simple data transformation, such as concatenation of character columns.
- **Using Transact-SQL statements to query a SQL Server database.**
  - Practice 1: Use SELECT statements to perform basic data access queries. Select all the columns in a table, and then restrict the returned results. Use the Northwind database shipped with SQL Server 2000 to practice writing different queries.
  - Practice 2: Use the SELECT statement to query more than one table using joins. Predefine the columns you will use to join the tables. After you have joined two tables, try to join three tables and then four tables.
  - Practice 3: Use subqueries nested in the WHERE clause of the SELECT statement. The subquery will return a single value to compare it with the outer query.

- Practice 4: Use a cursor to walk through the records in the recordset. Declare, open, close, and fetch data from a cursor. After closing the cursor, make sure you deallocate it.
- Practice 5: Use the statistical functions of Structured Query Language (SQL), such as COUNT, SUM, MIN, MAX, and AVG.

- **Using Transact-SQL to manipulate data in a SQL Server database.**
  - Practice 1: Use the INSERT statement to insert records into tables. It is necessary to view the schema definition of the table before inserting data. Take a close look at which columns require a value. Try to insert data without specifying each column. Also try to insert data without listing the columns in which you want to place data.
  - Practice 2: Use the UPDATE statement to update a record's columns. Try to use the WHERE clause to update more than one record in the database.
  - Practice 3: Use the DELETE statement to delete all the rows from a table. Use the WHERE clause to delete a set of records based on criteria requiring two joined tables.
- **Using cursors with a SQL Server database.**
  - Practice 1: Create cursors and familiarize yourself with their operations.
  - Practice 2: Create different types of cursors and examine their usage pattern.
  - Practice 3: Use cursors to manipulate data, including updating, inserting, and deleting rows.
- **Working with XML data.**
  - Practice 1: Retrieve XML data in different formats using the correct keyword, such as AUTO, RAW, or EXPLICIT.
  - Practice 2: Use OpenXML to open a rowset over a small XML document, selecting from the XML, and returning a result set.
  - Practice 3: Use XML queries via a URL and return data directly to the browser.

Further Reading

This section lists supplemental readings by objective. Study these sources thoroughly before taking exam 70-229.

Objective 3.1

Microsoft SQL Server 2000 product documentation. To access Books Online (BOL), click the Start button, point to Programs, then Microsoft SQL Server, and then click Books Online. Click the Contents tab and double-click the "Using the SQL Server Tools" topic. Then review "BCP Utility" under "Command Prompt Utilities."

Microsoft SQL Server 2000 product documentation. To access Books Online, click the Start button, point to Programs, then Microsoft SQL Server, and then click Books Online. Click the Contents tab, double-click "Data Transformation Services," and review "DTS Overview," "DTS Basics," and "DTS Tools."

Microsoft Corporation. *MCSE Training Kit: Microsoft SQL Server 2000 Database Design and Implementation*. Redmond, Washington: Microsoft Press, 2001. Read and complete the practices in Lesson 1, Chapter 7, "Managing and Manipulating Data."

Objective 3.2

Microsoft SQL Server 2000 product documentation. To access Books Online, click the Start button, point to Programs, then Microsoft SQL Server, and then click Books Online. Click the Contents tab and double-click "Accessing and Changing Relational Data."

Microsoft SQL Server 2000 product documentation. To access Books Online, click the Start button, point to Programs, then Microsoft SQL Server, and then click Books Online. Click the Contents tab and double-click the "Administering SQL Server" topic. Then review "Configuring Linked Servers" under "Managing Servers."

Microsoft SQL Server 2000 product documentation. To access Books Online, click the Start button, point to Programs, then Microsoft SQL Server, and then click Books Online. Click the Contents tab, double-click "SQL Server Architecture," and review "Distributed Query Architecture."

Delaney, Kalen. *Inside Microsoft SQL Server 2000*. Redmond, Washington: Microsoft Press, 2000. Review Chapter 7, "Querying Data."

Microsoft Corporation. *MCSE Training Kit: Microsoft SQL Server 2000 Database Design and Implementation*. Redmond, Washington: Microsoft Press, 2001. Read and complete the practices in Lesson 2, Chapter 7, "Managing and Manipulating Data."

Objective 3.3

Microsoft SQL Server 2000 product documentation. To access Books Online, click the Start button, point to Programs, then Microsoft SQL Server, and then click Books Online. Click the Contents tab, double-click "Accessing and Changing Relational Data," and review "Query Fundamentals," "Advanced Query Concepts," "Modifying Data," "Locking," "Cursors," and "Distributed Queries."

Delaney, Kalen. *Inside Microsoft SQL Server 2000*. Redmond, Washington: Microsoft Press, 2000. Review Chapter 7, "Querying Data.

Microsoft Corporation. *MCSE Training Kit: Microsoft SQL Server 2000 Database Design and Implementation*. Redmond, Washington: Microsoft Press, 2001. Read and complete the practices in Lessons 1, 2, and 3 in Chapter 6, "Accessing and Modifying Data."

Objective 3.4

Microsoft SQL Server 2000 product documentation. To access Books Online, click the Start button, point to Programs, then Microsoft SQL Server, and then click Books Online. Click the Contents tab, double-click "Accessing and Changing Relational Data," and review "Cursors."

Delaney, Kalen. *Inside Microsoft SQL Server 2000*. Redmond, Washington: Microsoft Press, 2000. Review Chapter 12, "Special Transact-SQL Operations: Working with Cursors and Large Objects."

Microsoft Corporation. *MCSE Training Kit: Microsoft SQL Server 2000 Database Design and Implementation*. Redmond, Washington: Microsoft Press, 2001. Read and complete the practices in Lessons 1, 2, and 3 in Chapter 6, "Accessing and Modifying Data," and Lesson 3 in Chapter 7, "Managing and Manipulating Data."

Objective 3.5

Microsoft SQL Server 2000 product documentation. To access Books Online, click the Start button, point to Programs, then Microsoft SQL Server, and then click Books Online. Click the Contents tab and double-click "XML and Internet Support."

Microsoft Corporation. *MCSE Training Kit: Microsoft SQL Server 2000 Database Design and Implementation*. Redmond, Washington: Microsoft Press, 2001. Read and complete the practices in Lesson 4, Chapter 7, "Managing and Manipulating Data."

OBJECTIVE 3.1

Import and export data.

Three main methods are provided by SQL Server 2000 to import and export data: the **BCP** utility, the **BULK INSERT** Transact-SQL command, and DTS.

The BCP utility is a fast method to import data from a file to a SQL Server table or view, or to export data from a SQL Server table, query, or view to a file. The BCP utility is the best choice when data is being moved from or to a file, and the move needs to be fast, with no transformations or other manipulations of any kind. The BCP operations might be logged, depending on a number of factors.

The BULK INSERT command is a regular Transact-SQL statement, much like the INSERT command, but it is used to insert data from a data file into a SQL Server table or view. BULK INSERT is significantly faster than BCP or DTS for text file imports. However, when importing native data, BCP performance is comparable to BULK INSERT performance. One of the main advantages of BULK INSERT is that it can be used within Transact-SQL and can be used within a transaction, allowing for rollback if needed.

DTS provides a very flexible and powerful framework for moving and transforming data and database objects. It has a number of wizards and tasks built in for importing and exporting data from multiple ODBC and OLE DB data sources. It provides a GUI to create complex workflows that can be saved and scheduled to be executed at another time. DTS allows data transformations to be included in the data movement tasks. These transformations can be written in VBScript or Microsoft JScript.

DTS exposes a **COM** object model that can be used with programming languages such as Microsoft Visual C++ or Microsoft Visual Basic to write more complex data transformation tasks within a program. DTS supplies an OLE DB provider called the **DTS Data Pump**, which exposes the interfaces and methods to move and transform data.

It is important to choose the appropriate tool for each data transfer need, to ensure flexibility as well as performance. However, with the three tools provided, there is very little that you cannot accomplish in data transfer.

Objective 3.1 Questions

70-229.03.01.001

You are about to bulk load a BCP export file into your database. You want the data to be loaded as quickly as possible. Which of the following must be met to ensure that your BCP load is as fast as possible?

A. Enable Select into/bulk copy.

B. The table cannot have an index.

C. The table can be replicated.

D. The filegroup of the database cannot have more than one file.

70-229.03.01.002

You need to import about a thousand rows of data from another system into a table on the production system. You want to be able to do this within a transaction that can be rolled back, if needed. This data must also be fully logged, and you need to ensure that all referential integrity on the table is checked, whether in constraints or triggers.

Which of the following approaches will best meet these requirements?

A. Use the BCP command-line utility to bulk copy the data with the FIRE_TRIGGERS and CHECK_CONSTRAINTS options.

B. Use the BCP command-line utility to bulk copy the data after setting the Select into/bulk copy database option.

C. Use the BULK INSERT command within a transaction with the FIRE_TRIGGERS and CHECK_CONSTRAINTS options.

D. Use the BULK INSERT command with the TABLOCK option.

70-229.03.01.003

Which of the following functions can be performed using DTS? (Choose all that apply.)

A. Move data between a SQL Server table and a Microsoft Access table, converting numeric data to character data.

B. Use File Transfer Protocol (FTP) to copy data from one location to another.

C. Use Message Queuing to split a large DTS job into smaller pieces and send the tasks to multiple computers.

D. Transfer logins and user-defined error messages from one server to another.

70-229.03.01.004

You are about to use DTS to load data from an Oracle database using Microsoft OLE-DB Provider for Oracle. What operations are valid? (Choose all that apply.)

A. Change the column data types.

B. Specify a query to retrieve a subset of the Oracle data.

C. Use JScript to write transformation scripts.

D. The destination table must be dropped and re-created before the data can be imported.

70-229.03.01.005

You want to export data from SQL Server to a text file. Which utilities can you use? (Choose all that apply.)

A. Use ISQL.

B. Use the DTS Export Wizard.

C. Use BCP.

Objective 3.1 Answers

70-229.03.01.001

► Correct Answers: A

A. **Correct:** This option must be enabled on your database to allow fast data load; however, the load has to fulfill other requirements. If you want all of your databases to have this option enabled when they are created, enable this option on your model database.

B. **Incorrect:** This answer is half true. You can have a table with indexes defined, but the table must be empty, or you can have a table with data but without indexes. If your table already has data and indexes, you should consider dropping the indexes, loading the data, and then re-creating the indexes.

C. **Incorrect:** If your table is participating in replication, you cannot perform a fast load, but you can still use BCP to load the data. The operation will be logged in the transaction log, and that will slow your database load.

D. **Incorrect:** The number of files in the database filegroup, or the filegroup in which the table is created, has no effect on the BCP operation.

70-229.03.01.002

► Correct Answers: C

A. **Incorrect:** The BCP utility cannot be run from within a transaction. It is a command-line utility that runs outside SQL Server. The FIRE_TRIGGERS option will force the INSERT TABLE triggers to fire, which by default are not fired. The CHECK_CONSTRAINTS option forces constraints to be checked, which are also ignored by default with a BCP operation. Also, the FIRE_TRIGGERS option will force the BCP operation to be fully logged.

B. **Incorrect:** The BCP utility cannot be run from within a transaction. It is a command-line utility that runs outside SQL Server. Setting the Select into/bulk copy database option can cause the operation to not be logged; however, if there are indexes on the table, or if it is being replicated, it will be logged. Because the FIRE_TRIGGERS and CHECK_CONSTRAINTS options were not set, referential integrity will not be checked.

C. **Correct:** BULK INSERT is a Transact-SQL command that can be run within a transaction and rolled back if needed. The FIRE_TRIGGERS options will force the INSERT TABLE triggers to fire, which by default are not fired. The CHECK_CONSTRAINTS option forces constraints to be checked, which are also ignored by default. Also, the FIRE_TRIGGERS option ensures that the operation is fully logged.

D. **Incorrect:** The BULK INSERT command can be used in a Transact-SQL transaction, but the TABLOCK option will cause only the table to be locked for the duration of the operation. Because triggers are not fired and constraints not checked by default, the referential integrity will not be checked.

70-229.03.01.003

▶ Correct Answers: A, B, C, and D

A. **Correct:** With DTS, Data can be moved between SQL Server and Access.

B. **Correct:** The built-in DTS File Transfer Protocol Task will allow files to be copied from one location to another, as well as entire directories.

C. **Correct:** Message Queuing can be used to send and receive messages between DTS packages for asynchronous processing. Messages can be received by multiple computers to perform different tasks. However, Message Queuing cannot take part in a DTS transaction.

D. **Correct:** The built-in DTS Transfer Logins Task can be used to transfer logins from one system to another, and the built-in Transfer Error Messages Task will transfer any error messages that have been added to the system with the sp_addmessage system stored procedure.

70-229.03.01.004

▶ Correct Answers: A, B, and C

A. **Correct:** You can convert from almost any SQL Server data type to any other data type. If simple conversion is not available, you can always write a script to transform the data.

B. **Correct:** If the data source driver or database supports SQL, you can always specify a SELECT statement to retrieve data.

C. **Correct:** SQL Server allows you to use VBScript or JScript to write your data transformation script.

D. **Incorrect:** You can import data into an existing table, or you can ask DTS to drop it for you. If the table does not exist, DTS will create it for you.

70-229.03.01.005

▶ Correct Answers: B and C

A. **Incorrect:** ISQL is a command-based query utility. It is used to execute batched jobs from the command line. You can use DTS Export Wizard or BCP to accomplish this task.

B. **Correct:** SQL Server includes a service called Data Transformation Services (DTS). DTS is used to transfer data to and from SQL Server from different data sources, such as ODBC, OLE DB, or text files. DTS allows you to specify the data you want to export and the format. You can also save the job in a package and reuse it at a later time.

C. **Correct:** BCP is a command-line utility used to import and export data in a native SQL Server format or in text format. BCP is used to transfer large amounts of data. BCP uses the ODBC API Bulk Copy interface, whereas earlier versions of BCP used DB-Library's bulk copy API.

OBJECTIVE 3.2

Manipulate heterogeneous data.

SQL Server 2000 offers a number of ways to manipulate external data from data sources other than SQL Server. These can include ODBC data sources, OLE DB data sources, and XML documents. They can also include Oracle databases, Access databases, Microsoft Excel files, and flat files.

The five main methods to manipulate heterogeneous data and produce distributed queries are as follows:

- **Linked servers**—Servers can be added as remote servers and then given a name that can be used within regular Transact-SQL statements. Objects on remote linked servers are identified by fully qualifying the object names, following the standard of server.database.owner.table.
- **OPENQUERY**—Allows a named server that is already identified as a linked server with the sp_addlinkedserver system stored procedure to be queried as a table within a Transact-SQL statement. A query to be run against the remote server is supplied and returns a result set to the calling server.
- **OPENDATASOURCE**—Allows a remote table to be opened by supplying ad hoc connection information in place of a table reference in a Transact-SQL statement. This function should be used only for infrequent queries against OLE DB data sources that are not defined as a linked server.
- **OPENROWSET**—Returns the result of a supplied query, as opposed to the entire table. Over a network, this method can be more efficient, and allows some of the work to be performed on the remote query. This allows a disparate data source to be accessed as a table in a Transact-SQL statement by indicating the connection parameters, as well as passing a statement that is run against the remote server, returning the result sets to the calling server.
- **OPENXML**—Allows a small XML document to have a rowset opened over it, with the results returned as a table and included in a Transact-SQL statement.

There are limitations in what statements can be used in a distributed query, depending on the capabilities of the remote server, and the type of query being written. Stored procedures can be run only against other SQL Server data sources. In general, SQL Server tries to run the remote query on the remote server, returning only the result sets to the calling server, to limit network traffic.

Note OPENDATASOURCE and OPENROWSET are actually **macros**, and do not allow any parameters. They also do not provide metadata for the remote results.

Objective 3.2 Questions

70-229.03.02.001

You need to create a one-time ad hoc distributed query against a remote computer running SQL Server. You have the connection string and the query. Which of the following rowset functions would be the best approach for this need?

A. Parse the connection string and add a linked server using the sp_addlinkedserver system stored procedure. Then write the query using the fully qualified, four-part object name.

B. Parse the connection string and add a linked server using the sp_addlinkedserver system. You can then use the OPENQUERY rowset function, supplying the linked server name and the query.

C. Use the OPENROWSET function, supplying the connection string and the query statement.

D. Use the DTS wizard to create a table and import the data from the other data source. Then run the query against the imported table.

70-229.03.02.002

You currently have all of your customer data in four separate servers, with the data partitioned by region. You want to be able to create a partitioned view for the Customers table that contains the SELECT…UNION ALL syntax for each of the four servers. This solution provides an abstraction layer for your client applications, so that developers do not need to know which physical server contains the required results. This solution also allows flexibility in the physical partitioning of the data because the implementation is hidden from the client users. Which of the following heterogeneous access methods will best support these requirements?

A. Add linked servers for each of the three remote servers on each server. Then create the view using the four-part, fully qualified object name in the SELECT…UNION ALL syntax.

B. Add linked servers for each of the three remote servers on each server. Then create the view using the OPENQUERY clause in the SELECT…UNION ALL syntax.

C. Create the partitioned view on each server using the OPENROWSET function in the SELECT...UNION ALL syntax, supplying the connection string for each of the three remote servers.

D. Create the partitioned view on each server using the OPENDATASOURCE clause in the SELECT...UNION ALL syntax, supplying the connection string for each of the three remote servers.

70-229.03.02.003

You need to query data from a large Access table without setting up a linked server. You want to filter the data in Access with a query before it is returned to the server. Which of the following approaches will best meet these requirements?

A. Use the OPENQUERY function.

B. Use the OPENXML function.

C. Use the OPENDATASOURCE function.

D. Use the OPENROWSET function.

Objective 3.2 Answers

70-229.03.02.001

▶ Correct Answers: C

A. **Incorrect:** Although you could parse the connection string to get the server name, this would be more work than necessary. Creating a linked server is also too much overhead for a one-time ad hoc query against a remote SQL Server.

B. **Incorrect:** Although you could parse the connection string to get the server name, this would be more work than necessary. Creating a linked server is also too much overhead for a one-time ad hoc query against a remote computer running SQL Server. The OPENQUERY clause does use a linked server name, but again, defining a linked server is too much overhead.

C. **Correct:** The OPENROWSET function is good for a one-time ad hoc distributed query. It doesn't require the overhead of adding a linked server, and it takes connection information and a remote query as parameters. OPENROWSET does not allow variables for any parameters and it will return only the first result set if the query returns multiple result sets.

D. **Incorrect:** This would work for a long-term solution, but creating a new table and DTS task and then importing the data is too much work and overhead for a one-time distributed query. It would also be extremely resource-intensive if the data set were large.

70-229.03.02.002

▶ Correct Answers: A

A. **Correct:** This solution is the best. Although OPENROWSET and OPENDATASOURCE can in some situations be used to create partitioned views, they are not the best approach because they are not as functional as linked servers. The overhead of creating a linked server is justified because the Customer partitioned view will be used often.

B. **Incorrect:** Although this would work, once linked servers are added, using the four-part, fully qualified object name is more understandable and easier to use than the OPENQUERY function. OPENQUERY provides no added functionality or performance in this situation.

C. **Incorrect:** Using OPENROWSET requires a connection string and does not support all of the functionality of linked servers.

D. **Incorrect:** Using OPENDATASOURCE requires a connection string and does not support all of the functionality of linked servers. It also does not allow a query to be supplied.

70-229.03.02.003

► Correct Answers: D

A. **Incorrect:** OPENQUERY requires a linked server, so using it does not meet all the requirements. You specify a query with OPENQUERY, so the result set would be limited to only the requested rows.

B. **Incorrect:** OPENXML requires an XML document for input, and although the data could be returned programmatically from the other servers as XML, this would be extremely limited and clumsy. Because XML is not required in this scenario, there is no need for it or major benefit from using it.

C. **Incorrect:** Although the OPENDATASOURCE function does not require a linked server, and it takes a connection string, it does not allow a query to limit the results returned from the remote provider. Therefore, more data than might be required would be returned. This does not meet the requirement.

D. **Correct:** This is the best solution. Using the OPENROWSET function with a query to limit the returned results would best meet the requirements. OPENROWSET also requires a connection string, not a linked server name.

OBJECTIVE 3.3

Retrieve, filter, group, summarize, and modify data by using Transact-SQL.

The **INSERT** statement is used to enter new rows into a database table. INSERT has three major parts: specifying the target table, specifying the columns where you want to place data, and specifying the values for those columns.

The **UPDATE** statement is used to update from one to many records in a database table. It also has three parts: specifying the target table, specifying the columns and their new values, and using the WHERE clause to specify the records to be modified. More complex UPDATE statements can have joins to specify the set of records to be updated.

The **DELETE** statement is used to delete one or more records from a database table. It has two parts: first, specifying the target table, and second, using the WHERE clause, specifying the records to be deleted. DELETE has the same capability as UPDATE to use joins to specify records to be deleted.

The **SELECT** statement is used to retrieve data from a database. You can indicate that you want all columns from the table returned or specify which columns you want returned. The FROM clause specifies the table or tables from which the data should be returned. The WHERE clause can contain a list of expressions to allow you to filter the results returned. Transact-SQL provides many conditional operators, such as AND, OR, BETWEEN, LIKE, IN, >, <, <>, =, >=, and <=. You can use DISTINCT to eliminate duplicate records.

The SELECT statement can be used to insert data into another table. The INSERT…SELECT statement can be used to add records to an existing table.

TOP can be used to specify the maximum number of records to be returned. By also using PERCENT you can specify a percentage of records to be returned.

Aggregation results are obtained by using the **MIN**, **MAX**, **COUNT**, **AVG**, **CUBE**, and **ROLLUP** functions to calculate the processed result set.

GROUP BY can be used to divide the table into groups. Groups can consist of columns, results, and computed columns.

ORDER BY is used to specify the sequencing of the returned result set. ORDER BY is invalid in views, inline functions, subqueries, and derived tables unless TOP is specified.

In this objective, you should have a good working knowledge of the INSERT, UPDATE, DELETE, and SELECT statements.

Objective 3.3 Questions

70-229.03.03.001

You have two computers running SQL Server named SERVER1 and SERVER2. Both of them have a SALES database with the same database schema. Which line of the following query will return an error when used as a distributed query against these servers?

```
SELECT c.CustomerID, COUNT(*) FROM
SERVER1.SALES..Customers c,
SERVER2.SALES.dbo.Orders o
WHERE c.CustomerID = o.CustomerID
GROUP BY c.CustomerID
```

A. `SERVER1.SALES..Customers c`

B. `SERVER2.SALES.dbo.Orders o`

C. `WHERE c.CustomerID = o.CustomerID`

D. `GROUP BY c.CustomerID`

70-229.03.03.002

You execute the following SQL statement:

```
SELECT CustomerID, COUNT(*) FROM Orders GROUP BY CustomerID HAVING COUNT(*) > 10
```

What result will SQL Server generate?

A. Incorrect syntax. You cannot use HAVING and COUNT together.

B. Incorrect syntax. You have to alias COUNT(*), and then you can use it in the HAVING clause.

C. Correct syntax. It will return all the records where COUNT(*) is greater than 10.

D. Incorrect syntax. The COUNT(*) must be in the GROUP BY column list.

70-229.03.03.003

You have the following statement:

```
SELECT TOP 10 ProductName,UnitPrice FROM Products ORDER BY UnitPrice DESC
```

Which of the following statements is true?

A. This statement returns the top 10 percent of the records, ordered by the UnitPrice.

B. This statement returns the first 10 rows, ordered by the UnitPrice in descending order.

C. You will receive an error message. All columns specified in the SELECT list must be in ORDER BY, just as with GROUP BY.

70-229.03.03.004

You want to decrease the price of 10 percent of the most expensive data in your inventory. Which Transact-SQL statement will do that?

A.
```
UPDATE Products
SET UnitPrice = UnitPrice * 0.9
WHERE ProductID = ( SELECT TOP 10 ProductID FROM Products ORDER BY UnitPrice DESC)
```

B.
```
UPDATE Products
SET UnitPrice = UnitPrice * 0.9
WHERE ProductID IN ( SELECT TOP 10 ProductID FROM Products ORDER BY UnitPrice DESC)
```

C.
```
UPDATE Products
SET UnitPrice = UnitPrice * 0.9
WHERE ProductID IN ( SELECT TOP 10 PERCENT ProductID FROM Products ORDER BY UnitPrice
DESC)
```

D.
```
UPDATE Products
SET UnitPrice = UnitPrice * .9
FROM Product a,Products b
WHERE a.ProductId = b.ProductId ORDER BY a.UnitPrice DESC TOP 10 PERCENT
```

70-229.03.03.005

Evaluate the following statement:

```
SELECT 4 / 4 + 2 * 5 - 5
```

Which operator will be evaluated first?

A. The addition operator will be evaluated first.

B. The multiplication operator will be evaluated first.

C. The subtraction operator will be evaluated third.

D. The division operator will be evaluated first.

70-229.03.03.006

Evaluate the following script:

```
DECLARE @rows INT, @errors INT
SELECT 5, 10, 15
IF @@ERROR > 0
     SET @errors = 1
ELSE
     SET @errors = 0
IF @@ROWCOUNT > 0
     SET @rows = @@ ROWCOUNT
ELSE
     SET @rows = -9999
SELECT @errors, @rows
```

What will be in the result set?

A. 0, -9999

B. 0, 0

C. 1, 1

D. 1, -9999

70-229.03.03.007

You have a SELECT statement that joins a table on a local server to a table on a linked server. The linked server has much more memory and processors than the local server. How can you ensure that the optimizer performs the join operation on the linked server?

A. Write the join as an OUTER join on the side that references the table on the linked server.

B. Use the fully qualified name for the linked server table.

C. Use the REMOTE table hint in the SELECT statement.

D. Use the MERGE join table hint in the SELECT statement.

70-229.03.03.008

You need to retrieve results from a table of employees that includes a NOT NULL EmployeeID column, a NULL Name column, and a NOT NULL Salary column.

- The required result is the sum of all of the employee salaries.
- The first optional result is the number of rows in the table.
- The second optional result is to return the largest salary.

You create the following Transact-SQL query:

```
SELECT SUM(Salary), COUNT(Name) from Employee
```

Which result will this query provide?

A. The required result and all optional results.

B. The required result and one optional result.

C. The required result and none of the optional results.

D. The query does not provide the required result.

70-229.03.03.009

You are designing a sales database application that will require the use of many transactions to ensure data consistency. You will deploy this application with many users, and you want to ensure that it is as scalable as possible. Which of the following will help to ensure that blocking is kept to a minimum, ensuring scalability? (Choose all that apply.)

A. Allow user input inside a transaction.

B. Keep transactions short and in small batches.

C. Use as low a level of transaction isolation as is allowable.

D. Use NOLOCK hints in SELECT statements where allowable.

70-229.03.03.010

How can using a stored procedure to insert data into the OrderDetails table reduce network traffic and increase database performance?

A. The number of requests between the server and the client is reduced.

B. The execution plan is stored in the cache after it was executed the first time.

C. Stored procedures accept parameters.

D. You can bypass permission checking on stored procedures.

Objective 3.3 Answers

70-229.03.03.001

► Correct Answers: A

A. **Correct:** This line is incorrect. You have to specify the object owner when using distributed queries. The correct syntax is server.database.owner.table.

B. **Incorrect:** This line is correct and well formed.

C. **Incorrect:** This line is correct. It is a well-formed condition used to build a join between the two referenced tables.

D. **Incorrect:** This line is correct. For the GROUP BY to be valid, you must have the column name listed in the SELECT part of the query.

70-229.03.03.002

► Correct Answers: C

A. **Incorrect:** You can use COUNT with HAVING; the only requirement is that the COUNT must be in the column list of the SELECT statement.

B. **Incorrect:** You can use the COUNT alias in the columns list of the SELECT statement, but you cannot use the alias in the HAVING clause.

C. **Correct:** This statement is correctly formed. The correct column names and expressions are in the SELECT statement. GROUP BY and HAVING are well formed statements.

D. **Incorrect:** You cannot use an aggregate in the GROUP BY clause. COUNT(*) must be listed in the columns list of the SELECT statement, but not in the columns list of the GROUP BY.

70-229.03.03.003

▶ Correct Answers: B

A. **Incorrect:** This statement will return the first 10 records from the Products table, ordered by the Unit-Price in a descending order. If you need to return the top 10 percent, use SELECT TOP 10 PER-CENT. DESC causes the ordering to be descending, from high to low.

B. **Correct:** TOP specifies the number of rows to return. ORDER BY and DESC cause the result set to be ordered in high-to-low UnitPrice order.

C. **Incorrect:** ORDER BY does not work the same way as GROUP BY. You can base ordering on one or more columns. Columns used in ORDER BY do not have to be in the SELECT column list. The following code would execute correctly: SELECT TOP 10 ProductName FROM Products ORDER BY UnitPrice DESC.

70-229.03.03.004

▶ Correct Answers: C

A. **Incorrect:** This answer is wrong because you needed to return the top 10 percent of the most expensive items. You should have used TOP 10 PERCENT instead of TOP 10. Also, the WHERE clause has a problem: if your subquery returns more than one row, you have to use IN; otherwise, the query will fail.

B. **Incorrect:** This query will execute successfully, but it won't provide the required result. You should have updated the top 10 percent of the most expensive items; instead, you updated the top 10 most expensive items.

C. **Correct:** This Transact-SQL statement will produce the required result.

D. **Incorrect:** If you update a table using UPDATE…FROM, you cannot use ORDER BY. ORDER BY can be used only with the SELECT statement. TOP 10 PERCENT is also usable only with a SELECT statement and must follow the SELECT keyword.

70-229.03.03.005

► Correct Answers: D

A. **Incorrect:** The addition operator will be evaluated third.

B. **Incorrect:** The multiplication operator will be evaluated second.

C. **Incorrect:** The subtraction operator will be evaluated fourth.

D. **Correct:** Like most languages, SQL Server 2000 has an operator precedence in which multiple operators can be used within one expression. Multiplication and division are evaluated before addition and subtraction. Operators with the same order of precedence are evaluated left to right. This statement will be evaluated as follows:

```
SELECT (((4 / 4) + (2 * 5)) - 5)
```

70-229.03.03.006

► Correct Answers: B

A. **Incorrect:** -9999 can never be returned from the @rows local variable because the @@ROWCOUNT global variable has been reset at the IF statement.

B. **Correct:** There are no errors in this statement because it is a simple SELECT statement using constants, so the @@ERROR global variable will return 0. However, because the IF statement always resets the results of the @@ROWCOUNT global variable to 0, the value of the @rows local variable can never be evaluated to -9999, but will always return 0.

C. **Incorrect:** There are no errors in the SELECT statement, so 1 will not be returned for the @errors local variable and, because of the reset of the @@ROWCOUNT global variable after the IF statement, 1 will never be returned from the @rows local variable.

D. **Incorrect:** There are no errors in the SELECT statement, so 1 will not be returned for the @errors local variable. The script never enters the ELSE clause for the @rows local variable because the @@ROWCOUNT global variable has been reset after the first IF statement, so -9999 will never be returned.

70-229.03.03.007

► Correct Answers: C

A. **Incorrect:** An OUTER join indicates a type of join, not the location of the join operation being performed. This solution has other problems because the result set from an OUTER join is different from the result set from an INNER join.

B. **Incorrect:** Using fully qualified names does not affect where the actual join operation will be performed.

C. **Correct:** Using the REMOTE hint will force the optimizer to perform the actual join operation on the remote server. This can be used only with an INNER join, and the remote table should be on the right side of the join.

D. **Incorrect:** The MERGE hint forces the optimizer to use the merge algorithm for performing the join. It does not determine where the actual operation will be performed.

70-229.03.03.008

► Correct Answers: C

A. **Incorrect:** The proposed query satisfies only the required result.

B. **Incorrect:** The proposed query satisfies only the required result.

C. **Correct:** The query returns the sum of all of the salaries in the table with the use of the SUM function. There is a COUNT function to return the number of rows in the table, but it will not return an accurate number because the Name column is used as the input for the COUNT function. Because the Name column will allow null values, the COUNT function will count only the rows that have a value for the Name column. The asterisk (*) should always be used with the COUNT function if the number of rows in the table is the desired result, regardless of null values in specific columns. Also, there is no function to return the largest salary value from the table. The MAX function could have been used, with the Salary column as input to provide this result.

D. **Incorrect:** The proposed query satisfies the required result.

70-229.03.03.009

▶ Correct Answers: B, C, and D

A. **Incorrect:** It is critical to not allow user input inside a transaction. You have no control over how long a user will keep that transaction open if input is required. The user might go to lunch, leaving the transaction open and the locks held against the tables used in the transaction. It is best to collect user input before the transaction begins.

B. **Correct:** Keeping the transaction and batch size small will ensure that locks are held for a minimal time and allow other users to get access to the resources. This is critical to ensure database scalability.

C. **Correct:** Setting the transaction isolation level to a lower level than the default of READ COMMITTED can help to keep locking at a minimum. The READ COMMITTED level, which is the SQL Server 2000 default, holds shared locks to ensure that there are no dirty reads, but data can be changed by another user in the middle of a transaction, which can cause phantoms and nonrepeatable reads. Setting the level to READ UNCOMMITTED means that no shared locks are acquired and exclusive locks are not honored. This is the lowest and least intrusive isolation level, but it must be used only in appropriate situations. This has the same effect as using the NOLOCK hint in a SELECT statement.

D. **Correct:** The NOLOCK hint in the SELECT statement is an excellent way to minimize locking in transactions where it is appropriate. It will take any locks on the tables included in the SELECT statement.

70-229.03.03.010

▶ Correct Answers: A and B

A. **Correct:** Stored procedures are a collection of Transact-SQL Statements. You do not have to send the statements down to the server one by one. The code is kept on the server side, just the parameters have to be sent to the server.

B. **Correct:** The first time a stored procedure is executed a plan is created. The compiled plan is then placed into the procedure cache. Subsequent execution of the stored procedure will be faster because the compiled plan is already in cache.

C. **Incorrect:** Although stored procedures accept parameters, this process does not reduce network traffic and does not increase performance.

D. **Incorrect:** In SQL Server, you cannot bypass permission and security checking for any kind of object. Stored procedures yield improved performance because the Transact-SQL code does not have to be sent down to the server, and the stored procedure execution plan can be cached on the server side after it was executed once.

OBJECTIVE 3.4

Manage result sets by using cursors and Transact-SQL.

A SELECT statement with a WHERE clause will return only those records that satisfy the WHERE condition. This complete set of rows is known as a **result set**.

Transact-SQL cursors are an extension of the result set, and they provide ways to manipulate the result set one row at a time. Cursors provide the way to "walk" the result set forward and backward. The cursor acts as a pointer in the result set, pointing at a specific row. The cursor also provides ways to modify the data in the rows and support different levels of visibility of changes made by other users.

In SQL Server 2000, you can use cursors in two different ways. The first is using Transact-SQL, and the second is using the API cursor functions. All cursors require temporary resources in the cache. These resources can include memory, paging files, temporary files, or databases. Large cursors or unnecessary cursors can degrade the performance of SQL Server.

SQL Server supports three different types of cursors: static, dynamic, and keyset.

- Static cursors return a result set that is a snapshot of the data when the recordset is opened. Changes made to the membership, order, and data values in the database after the result set is returned are not visible in the static result set.
- Dynamic cursors return a result set that is the opposite of the static result set. All changes made to the membership, order, and data values of the rows in the result set are visible when you scroll through the result set.
- Keyset cursors return a result set that is controlled by a unique set of identifiers known as the keyset. As in a static result set, the membership and order are fixed at the time of the opening of the result set. The keyset is kept in the tempdb database.

SQL Server also supports forward-only cursors. Forward-only cursors are defined by the FORWARD_ONLY keyword, which can be applied to all three result set types. Forward-only cursors use resources more efficiently than scrolling cursors do. However, forward-only cursors allow only forward fetches.

For this objective you should know the differences between the different cursors. You should understand the differences in their behavior.

Objective 3.4 Questions

70-229.03.04.001

You need to create a cursor that reflects the changes made to the database table even after the result set is returned. Which cursor type would you use?

A. FORWARD_ONLY

B. Static

C. Keyset

D. Dynamic

E. FAST_FORWARD

70-229.03.04.002

You need to define a cursor. Which statement should you use?

A. DECLARE CURSOR

B. OPEN

C. FETCH

D. @@FETCH_STATUS

70-229.03.04.003

Evaluate this statement:

```
DECLARE MyCursor CURSOR
STATIC LOCAL FOR
SELECT ZipCode from ZipCodes where State='NV'
```

Which of the following is true about this statement?

A. The result set is updateable globally.

B. The result set is stored in the tempdb database and all changes made by other users are reflected in your result set.

C. The cursor can be used by other subsequent operations in different stored procedures.

D. The result set is stored in the tempdb database and available only in the current stored procedure.

Objective 3.4 Answers

70-229.03.04.001

► Correct Answers: D

A. **Incorrect:** FORWARD_ONLY is not a cursor type but rather is an option that you can use with static, keyset, or dynamic cursors. If you use FORWARD_ONLY without a cursor type specification, you will have a forward-only dynamic cursor.

B. **Incorrect:** A static cursor makes a copy of the data used by the cursor. All requests to the cursor are fulfilled from a temporary table in the tempdb database. All requests come from a copy of the original data, so changes made to the original data will not be visible in the temporary table.

C. **Incorrect:** For a keyset cursor, SQL Server builds a temporary table in the tempdb database with a set of keys that uniquely identify each record. Changes made by you or by other users will be visible to you while you are moving forward or backward in the table.

D. **Correct:** A dynamic cursor reflects all changes in the recordset, and the values, orders, and membership of each row can change with each FETCH.

E. **Incorrect:** FAST_FORWARD is not a cursor type. FAST_FORWARD defines a FORWARD_ONLY and READ_ONLY cursor with performance optimization.

70-229.03.04.002

► Correct Answers: A

A. **Correct:** DECLARE CURSOR defines the attributes of a SQL Server cursor. The statement includes the SELECT statement and variables that the cursor uses. When you need to work with cursors, your first step should be to declare a cursor. Users must have SELECT permission on the table.

B. **Incorrect:** The OPEN statement is for opening and populating the cursor. The OPEN statement cannot define a cursor.

C. **Incorrect:** The FETCH statement is used to fetch the next or previous record from an already defined and open cursor. The FETCH statement can be executed only after the OPEN statement has been executed.

D. **Incorrect:** @@FETCH_STATUS is not a statement but is instead a global status variable. When cursors are used, you should check the last status of your fetch. The @@FETCH_STATUS variable has the following three possible status values: FETCH statement was successful, FETCH failed or the cursor point was beyond the result set, or the row fetched is missing.

70-229.03.04.003

▶ Correct Answers: D

A. **Incorrect:** This result set is declared with the LOCAL keyword. A local cursor is available only in the stored procedure where it was created. At the end of the stored procedure, these cursors are deallocated automatically, but you should always implement the necessary code to clean up after your cursor. Cursors declared with the GLOBAL keyword are available outside the scope of the current stored procedure.

B. **Incorrect:** Although the cursors will be allocated in the tempdb database, the scope of the cursor will be local to the stored procedure. LOCAL means that the cursor will be accessible only within the scope of the stored procedure.

C. **Incorrect:** A local cursor is available only within the scope of the stored procedure. If a cursor is required to be accessible within different stored procedures, you need to declare it as global using the GLOBAL keyword.

D. **Correct:** A static local cursor is allocated in the tempdb database and is available only within the scope of the stored procedure where it was declared.

OBJECTIVE 3.5

Extract data in XML format.

One of the new features in SQL Server 2000 is the ability to extract data in XML format. Results can be returned to a client in XML format by adding the FOR XML clause to the SELECT statement. You can also return result sets in XML format using templates and XPath queries. SQL Server 2000 can also be queried directly from a URL.

FOR XML returns results in a number of different ways, providing great flexibility. FOR XML is valid only for the SELECT statement, and its usage has a number of restrictions. It cannot be used within a view, with cursors, or with the COMPUTE BY or GROUP BY clauses, and it cannot be used in subqueries.

FOR XML can be used in the following ways:

- SELECT…FOR XML RAW—This returns each row in the result set as one element called "row," with columns indicated in the SELECT statement as attribute=value pairs. For example, the query `SELECT CUSTOMER.CUSTOMERNAME, ORDERS.ORDERID FROM CUSTOMER, ORDERS WHERE CUSTOMER.CUSTOMERID=ORDERS.CUSTOMERID` might return the following XML:

  ```
  <row CUSTOMERNAME="Brown" ORDERID="101" />
  <row CUSTOMERNAME="Brown" ORDERID="105" />
  <row CUSTOMERNAME="Yates" ORDERID="225" />
  ```

  Notice that the result is nonhierarchical and looks very much like the result sets you are used to in SQL Server. Because Brown has two orders, the name is returned twice.

- SELECT...FOR XML AUTO—This returns hierarchical data, depending on the number of tables in the join and the order of the columns. Generally, an element is created for each table, with the columns returned as attribute=value pairs. The same query as in the preceding example, `SELECT CUSTOMER.CUSTOMERNAME, ORDERS.ORDERID FROM CUSTOMER, ORDERS WHERE CUSTOMER.CUSTOMERID=ORDERS.CUSTOMERID`, would return the following XML:

```
<CUSTOMER CUSTOMERNAME="Brown" >
  <ORDERS ORDERID="101" />
  <ORDERS ORDERID="105" />
</CUSTOMER >

<CUSTOMER CUSTOMERNAME="Yates" >
  <ORDERS ORDERID="225" />
</CUSTOMER >
```

This hierarchical data return is very useful. Note that the column order in the SELECT clause is significant in determining the hierarchy.

- SELECT... FOR XML EXPLICIT—This option provides much more flexibility, but requires the query to be written in a specific way to produce the expected output. It is more functional than the RAW or AUTO clauses, but also more complicated. This option allows you to control what data is returned as elements and what is returned as attributes, which are fixed in the AUTO and RAW options.

- The XMLDATA option can be added to any of the SELECT statements described in this list to return an XML schema generated from the table structure. The schema will be returned before the actual results. XML schemas provide information about the table structure.

The entire XML functionality is implemented in Sqlxmlx.dll. When SQLOLEDB determines that the command is an XML command, the provider passes that command to Sqlxmlx.dll, which executes the command and returns the result to SQLOLEDB. There is obviously some overhead in producing XML. It is important to determine when it is necessary to extract data from SQL Server in XML format.

Objective 3.5 Questions

70-229.03.05.001

Evaluate the following XML result returned from a SELECT statement with the FOR XML option:

```
<row stor_name="Eric the Read Books" qty="5"/>
<row stor_name="Bookbeat" qty="10"/>
```

The following query was used to produce this result:

```
SELECT Stores.Stor_Name, Sales.Qty
FROM Stores JOIN Sales
ON Stores.Stor_ID = Sales.Stor_ID
WHERE Title_ID = 'BU1032'
```

Which FOR XML option was used to produce this output?

A. FOR XML RAW

B. FOR XML AUTO

C. FOR XML RAW, XMLDATA.

D. FOR XML AUTO, XMLDATA

70-229.03.05.002

You need to send an XML data stream to another business that will then use that data to create orders in its system. They do not want the data in hierarchical order, but they need to know the data types. Which of the FOR XML clauses would be best suited for these requirements?

A. FOR XML RAW

B. FOR XML AUTO

C. FOR XML RAW, XMLDATA

D. FOR XML AUTO, XMLDATA

70-229.03.05.003

Evaluate the following XML result returned from a SELECT statement with the FOR XML AUTO option:

```
<Stores Stor_Name="Eric the Read Books">
  <Sales Qty="3" Title_ID="1013">
    <Titles Title="Is Anger The Enemy?"/>
  </Sales>
</Stores>
<Stores Stor_Name="Doc-U-Mat: Quality Laundry and Books">
  <Sales Qty="20" Title_ID="1013">
    <Titles Title="Is Anger the Enemy?"/>
  </Sales>
  <Sales Qty="25" Title_ID="1043">
    <Titles Title="Life Without Fear"/>
  </Sales>
</Stores>
```

Which of the following queries was used to produce this result?

A. `SELECT Titles.Title, sales.Qty, Stores.Stor_Name, Sales.Title_id FROM Stores JOIN Sales ON Stores.Stor_ID = Sales.Stor_ID JOIN Titles ON Sales.Title_ID = Titles.Title_ID WHERE State = 'WA' FOR XML AUTO`

B. `SELECT sales.qty, sales.title_id, stores.stor_name, titles.title FROM stores JOIN sales ON stores.stor_id = sales.stor_id JOIN titles ON sales.title_id = titles.title_id WHERE state = 'WA' FOR XML AUTO`

C. `SELECT stores.stor_name, sales.qty, titles.title, sales.title_id FROM stores JOIN sales ON stores.stor_id = sales.stor_id JOIN titles ON sales.title_id = titles.title_id WHERE state = 'WA' FOR XML AUTO`

Objective 3.5 Answers

70-229.03.05.001

▶ Correct Answers: A

A. **Correct:** Because the XML RAW option displays *row* as the element name, we can determine that this was generated using the RAW option.

B. **Incorrect:** The AUTO option would have returned the element names as the table names.

C. **Incorrect:** Although this XML option has the generic row as the element name, this was generated by the RAW option. However, because there is no schema prefacing the results, this was not generated using the XMLDATA option.

D. **Incorrect:** The AUTO option returns the element names as the table names, and the XMLDATA would cause the schema to be generated and prepended to the results.

70-229.03.05.002

▶ Correct Answers: C

A. **Incorrect:** This clause produces the results in a nonhierarchical order, so RAW is the right approach, but there will not be any schema provided.

B. **Incorrect:** This clause produces the results in a hierarchical order, which does not meet the criteria. There will not be any schema provided.

C. **Correct:** This selection produces nonhierarchical data prefaced with the schema information, which meets the requirements.

D. **Incorrect:** Although this clause will produce the schema, because of the XMLDATA option, it will be returned in hierarchical order, which does not meet the requirements.

70-229.03.05.003

► Correct Answers: C

A. **Incorrect:** The hierarchy is determined by the order of the tables referenced in the columns in the SELECT statement. In the generated XML, the order of the elements is Stores, Sales, Titles—not Titles, Sales, Stores, Sales, as displayed in this query. Only the first occurrence of a table is used, and other occurrences are added as attributes to the table element.

B. **Incorrect:** The hierarchy is determined by the order of the tables referenced in the columns in the SELECT statement. In the generated XML, the order of the elements is stores, sales, titles—not sales, stores, titles as displayed in this query. Only the first occurrence of a table is used, and other occurrences are added as attributes to the table element.

C. **Correct:** In the generated XML, the order of the elements is stores, sales, titles, as displayed in this query. Only the first occurrence of a table is used, and other occurrences are added as attributes to the table element.

OBJECTIVE DOMAIN 4

Programming Business Logic

To access data in a Microsoft SQL Server database, you can use **Transact-SQL** statements. For complex tasks, this becomes repetitive and inefficient. You can address such tasks by creating **stored procedures**. A stored procedure is a precompiled collection of Transact-SQL statements kept as a unit under a unique name. Stored procedures are kept within the SQL Server database and can be executed with a single command. Stored procedures allow user-declared variables, groupings, conditional execution, and other programming features. Stored procedures can contain a group of statements and calls to other stored procedures. They can have input and output parameters. Stored procedures can also return status value and indicate success or failure.

A **transaction** is the basic unit for modifying data while preserving the ACID properties: atomicity, consistency, isolation, and durability. A transaction is a sequence of operations that is performed as a single unit of work.

- **Atomicity—**A transaction must be a single unit of work or modification completed or none.
- **Consistency—**When the transaction completes, the data will be in a consistent state. In a SQL Server database, this means that the data is valid, and that triggers, rules, and so on are processed without any errors. All internal structures are updated.
- **Isolation—**Transactions can be executed concurrently. Transactions must provide a total isolation from other transactions executed concurrently. If two transactions are accessing the same data, one transaction can see the data either before the other transaction begins or after, but not while the changes are being made.
- **Durability—**After the transaction is completed, all changes in the database are permanent and would survive system failure.

SQL Server supports three different kinds of transactions: **explicit transactions**, **implicit transactions**, and **distributed transactions**.

SQL Server uses different kinds of locks within the database to prevent conflicts. Locks make the serialization of transactions possible. SQL Server automatically selects the right kind of lock to the specific transaction. Locks ensure that data is being read and written cleanly.

To extend SQL Server Transact-SQL programmability, SQL Server 2000 provides user-defined functions. User-defined functions, like stored procedures, can encapsulate frequently used operations, but they can also return a scalar value or a table.

Tested Skills and Suggested Practices

The skills that you need to successfully master the Programming Business Logic objective domain on the *Designing and Implementing Databases with Microsoft SQL Server 2000 Enterprise Edition* exam include:

- **Using stored procedures to access, manipulate, and manage data in the database.**
  - Practice 1: Create stored procedures to access the database using the SELECT statement. Use parameters passed in to a stored procedure to specify the range of data you want to view.
  - Practice 2: Use stored procedures and cursors to manipulate data in tables.
  - Practice 3: Use stored procedures to insert a record into a database table. All column values should be passed into the stored procedure and inserted into a table.
  - Practice 4: Use the UPDATE statement within the stored procedure to update a table based on the passed-in values.
  - Practice 5: Write stored procedures with both input and output parameters.
- **Using triggers to enforce data integrity in a SQL Server database.**
  - Practice 1: Create an INSERT trigger on a SQL Server table. This trigger should insert another row into another table using the values available in the temporary "inserted" table.
  - Practice 2: Create an UPDATE trigger. If the values are not in the acceptable range, raise an error and roll back the transaction.

  - Practice 3: Create a DELETE trigger. Based on the values, update other tables.
  - Practice 4: Create INSTEAD OF triggers for INSERT, UPDATE, and DELETE operations on a table, and do the appropriate work for a table.
- **Using transactions to ensure data integrity.**
  - Practice 1: Insert, update, and delete data from different tables using transactional protection.
  - Practice 2: Use transaction and data manipulation, and then abort the transaction.
  - Practice 3: Use transaction savepoints and roll back to a savepoint.
  - Practice 4: Change the connection transaction behavior from the default, and look at the different behaviors.
- **Creating user-defined functions.**
  - Practice 1: Create a user-defined function that takes LastName, FirstName as varchars and returns a concatenation of both as varchar.
  - Practice 2: Return a table and use it in the FROM clause of a join.

Further Reading

This section lists supplemental readings by objective. Study these sources thoroughly before taking exam 70-229.

Objective 4.1

Microsoft SQL Server 2000 product documentation. To access Books Online (BOL), click the Start button, point to Programs, then Microsoft SQL Server, and click Books Online. Click the Contents tab and double-click the "SQL Server Architecture" topic. Then review "Transactions Architecture" under "Relational Database Engine Architecture."

Microsoft SQL Server 2000 product documentation. To access Books Online, click the Start button, point to Programs, then Microsoft SQL Server, and click Books Online. Click the Contents tab, double-click "Accessing and Changing Relational Data," and review "Accessing and Changing Data Fundamentals" and "Transactions."

Microsoft SQL Server 2000 product documentation. To access Books Online, click the Start button, point to Programs, then Microsoft SQL Server, and click Books Online. Click the Contents tab, double-click "Creating and Maintaining Databases," and review "Stored Procedures," "Views," "Enforcing Business Rules with Triggers," and "User-Defined Functions."

Microsoft Corporation. *MCSE Training Kit: Microsoft SQL Server 2000 Database Design and Implementation.* Redmond, Washington: Microsoft Press, 2001. Read and complete the practices in Lesson 3 in Chapter 2, "Using Transact-SQL on a SQL Server Database," Lessons 1, 2, and 3 in Chapter 8, "Implementing Stored Procedures," Lessons 1, 2, and 3 in Chapter 9, "Implementing Triggers," Lessons 1, 2, and 3 in Chapter 10, "Implementing Views," and Lessons 1, 2, and 3 in Chapter 12, "Managing SQL Server Transactions and Locks."

Objective 4.2

Microsoft SQL Server 2000 product documentation. To access Books Online, click the Start button, point to Programs, then Microsoft SQL Server, and then click Books Online. Click the Contents tab, double-click "Creating and Maintaining Databases," and review "Enforcing Business Rules with Triggers."

Microsoft SQL Server 2000 product documentation. To access Books Online, click the Start button, point to Programs, then Microsoft SQL Server, and click Books Online. Click the Contents tab and double-click the "Accessing and Changing Relational Data" topic. Then review "Advanced Query Concepts." Also review "Advanced Topics" under "Transactions."

Microsoft Corporation. *MCSE Training Kit: Microsoft SQL Server 2000 Database Design and Implementation.* Redmond, Washington: Microsoft Press, 2001. Read and complete the practices in Lesson 3 in Chapter 2, "Using Transact-SQL on a SQL Server Database," Lessons 1, 2, and 3 in Chapter 8, "Implementing Stored Procedures," Lessons 1, 2, and 3 in Chapter 9, "Implementing Triggers," Lessons 1, 2, and 3 in Chapter 10, "Implementing Views," and Lessons 1, 2, and 3 in Chapter 12, "Managing SQL Server Transactions and Locks."

Objective 4.3

Microsoft SQL Server 2000 product documentation. To access Books Online, click the Start button, point to Programs, then Microsoft SQL Server, and click Books Online. Click the Contents tab and double-click the "Accessing and Changing Relational Data" topic. Then review "Using Options in SQL Server" under "Accessing and Changing Data." Also review "Error Handling" under "Advanced Query Concepts."

Microsoft SQL Server 2000 product documentation. To access Books Online, click the Start button, point to Programs, then Microsoft SQL Server, and click Books Online. Click the Contents tab and double-click the "Using the SQL Server Tools" topic. Then double-click the "User Interface Reference" topic and review "Using Transact-SQL Debugger" under "SQL Query Analyzer Help."

Microsoft Corporation. *MCSE Training Kit: Microsoft SQL Server 2000 Database Design and Implementation*. Redmond, Washington: Microsoft Press, 2001. Read and complete the practices in Lesson 1, Chapter 14, "Maintaining and Optimizing SQL Server Database."

OBJECTIVE 4.1

Manage data manipulation by using stored procedures, transactions, triggers, user-defined functions, and views.

Data can be manipulated in special ways in SQL Server 2000 with stored procedures, transactions, triggers, user-defined functions, and views. Each of these methods is specialized for different uses, although their functionality might overlap in some ways.

Stored procedures are optimized for repeated usage in that the code can be created and tested, and when the code is first compiled, the execution plan will be saved for further use. One of the best ways to encapsulate known business code is to use stored procedures. By using stored procedures, you can also best ensure that the execution plan and the code will be reused. Stored procedures provide a logical abstraction layer. Using stored procedures can also help enforce some good programming habits, such as testing of SQL code, and ensuring that code is kept under source control. Client and middle-tier applications can be protected from changes to the underlying database objects when stored procedures are implemented because the procedures can be changed, with no code change to the outlying layers.

User-defined explicit transactions allow blocks of code to be handled together as one logical unit of work, with user-controlled rollback or commit.

Triggers are pieces of user-defined business logic that are fired whenever certain changes happen to a table. In SQL Server 2000, users can implement multiple AFTER triggers, which fire after a data manipulation command, as well as an INSTEAD OF trigger that will fire instead of (and hence, before) the data manipulation.

New to SQL Server 2000 are user-defined functions. These are functions that are created by the user and can be used inline in queries and to simplify coding. They provide a great deal of coding flexibility and the ability to encode some business logic in a simple-to-use function. User-defined functions can return scalar values or tables.

Views are logical abstractions over queries, commonly used to replace a complex query with a view that is easy to maintain and understand. SQL Server 2000 allows partitioned views, which provide a unioned view over multiple tables partitioned by some data constraint, as well as indexed views. Indexed views allow queries that are problematic from an optimization standpoint to be created and treated as a separate table, which the system manages, keeping it up to date when changes are made to the underlying base tables. A unique clustered index can then be created on the view, providing potentially huge performance gains. Indexed views are currently available only in the Enterprise Edition of SQL Server 2000.

Managing error handling in SQL Server code can be problematic because there is no built-in error handler. Generally, the best practice is to check the current results of the @@ERROR global variable after each statement, performing some error handling work dependent on the result. The global variable @@ROWS can also be used to determine whether any rows were affected by a statement. It is important to understand the scope of both of these variables because the next statement might immediately affect them, whether that statement returns results or not. For example, a common mistake is to run a SQL command, use the IF @@ROWCOUNT construct to check for the number of rows, and then to use the IF @@ERROR construct to check the error code and perform a function. However, the first IF statement resets the @@ERROR global variable to 0, negating the intended error-checking code.

Objective 4.1 Questions

70-229.04.01.001

In your stored procedure, you have to raise an error. What are the capabilities of RAISERROR? (Choose all that apply.)

A. It can print a message to the application.

B. It can assign an error number, state, and severity.

C. It can be logged in the error log.

D. The message string can contain substitution variables.

70-229.04.01.002

You are creating a stored procedure that will call a number of other stored procedures. If any of the inside stored procedures do not complete the required business logic, the outer stored procedure should stop execution with a message to the user. It does not need to roll back the previous work. Which of the following approaches will meet these requirements?

A. In the outer stored procedure, use a SELECT statement to check the results of @@ERROR after each inner stored procedure. If the result is zero, continue; otherwise, return an error message and stop execution.

B. Inside each inner stored procedure, store an error number as a return result from the stored procedure. In the outer stored procedure, check the result code of the inner stored procedure and continue if there is no error; otherwise, return an error message and stop execution.

C. Create a transaction inside the outer stored procedure that wraps each of the inner stored procedures. In the outer stored procedure, use a SELECT statement to check the results of @@ROWCOUNT after the execution of each inner stored procedure. If the result is zero, continue; otherwise, return an error message and stop execution.

D. In the outer stored procedure, use a SELECT statement to check the result of @@ROWCOUNT after the execution of each inner stored procedure. If the result is not zero, continue; otherwise, return an error message and stop execution.

70-229.04.01.003

Which of the following statements can cause a transaction to roll back if you have set XACT_ABORT on? (Choose all that apply.)

A. ROLLBACK TRAN

B. RAISERROR

C. In a statement, you use WHERE 1/0 and cause a divide by zero error.

D. PRINT

70-229.04.01.004

You want to create a user-defined function to parse a telephone number passed to the user-defined function. You want the return value to be a table, and if the value is invalid, you want to abort the current transaction. Which of the following statements is true?

A. You can use ROLLBACK TRAN and you can return a table.

B. You cannot use ROLLBACK TRAN and cannot return a table.

C. You can use ROLLBACK, but you cannot return a table.

D. You cannot use ROLLBACK, but you can return a table.

70-229.04.01.005

You created a partitioned view, and now you want to override the INSERT, UPDATE, and DELETE statement behavior. Which of the following statements are true?

A. You cannot use an INSTEAD OF trigger on a partitioned view.

B. You can use an AFTER trigger only on a partitioned view.

C. You can use INSTEAD OF triggers, but each type (INSERT, UPDATE, and DELETE) can have only one definition.

D. You can use INSTEAD OF triggers on tables and views in place of INSERT, UPDATE, and/or DELETE triggers.

70-229.04.01.006

You need to add business logic to an INSERT trigger to add the row to an audit table in another database for every INSERT in one table. This table has an IDENTITY column for the primary key, and the table has two triggers, one that also inserts into another table the current rows inserted. What is the best way to get the value of the identity column just inserted?

A. In the trigger, use a SELECT statement to save the value of @@IDENTITY after the INSERT statement and use this value to insert the row into the audit table.

B. In the trigger, use a SELECT statement to check the return value of the SCOPE_IDENTITY function after the INSERT statement.

C. In the trigger, use a SELECT statement to check the return value of the IDENT_CURRENT function, passing in the name of the table as the parameter after the INSERT statement, and use this value to insert the row into the audit table.

70-229.04.01.007

You need to create a stored procedure to return one calculated value converted to a string value. Which of the following methods will best produce the results you want?

A. You create the stored procedure declaring a varchar variable as output and use a SELECT statement to store the converted result into this variable.

B. Use a SELECT statement to check the value in @@ROWS after the stored procedure execution.

C. Return the result as a return code from the stored procedure.

D. Use a SELECT statement to check the result in the stored procedure.

70-229.04.01.008

You have a database that includes all of the company's employees. You currently have Employee and Job tables, which relate an employee to a manager through the Job table. The Employee table contains the rows for all employees, including managers. There is also a flag called Current in the Job table that indicates the current job for an employee. There is a constraint on the table that ensures that only one row can be indicated as the Current job for each employee. You would like to create a simple way to return an employee's current manager's ID. The approach should be flexible enough to be used in any command, including the BCP utility, if needed. Which of the following code snippets would best satisfy these requirements?

A.
```
CREATE FUNCTION CurrentManager  (@EmployeeID int) RETURNS int AS BEGIN
DECLARE @ManagerID int
SELECT @ ManagerID =Job.ManagerID
FROM Employee JOIN Job on Employee.EmployeeID = Job.EmployeeID
JOIN Employee as Manager ON Job.ManagerID = Manager.EmployeeID
WHERE Employee.EmployeeID = @EmployeeID
AND Job.CurrentJob = 1
RETURN @ ManagerID
END
```

B.
```
CREATE VIEW CurrentManager AS
SELECT Job.ManagerID
FROM Employee JOIN Job on Employee.EmployeeID = Job.EmployeeID
JOIN Employee as Manager ON Job.ManagerID = Manager.EmployeeID
WHERE Job.CurrentJob = 1
```

C.
```
CREATE PROCEDURE CurrentManager  (@employeeid int) AS
BEGIN
SELECT Job.ManagerID
FROM Employee JOIN Job on Employee.EmployeeID = Job.EmployeeID
JOIN Employee as Manager ON Job.ManagerID = Manager.EmployeeID
WHERE Employee.EmployeeID = @employeeid
AND Job.CurrentJob = 1
END
```

70-229.04.01.009

You have a stored procedure that will require nested transactions to ensure that all modifications are applied. You want to ensure that there are no transactions open at the completion of the stored procedure. Which of the following global variables can be interrogated to determine if a transaction is still open?

A. @@CONNECTIONS

B. @@NESTLEVEL

C. @@.FETCH_STATUS

D. @@TRANCOUNT

Objective 4.1 Answers

70-229.04.01.001

► Correct Answers: A, B, C, and D

A. **Correct:** RAISERROR can send a message to the application just like the PRINT function, but it has more options than PRINT.

B. **Correct:** RAISERROR can assign the specific error, severity, and state numbers.

C. **Correct:** RAISERROR can request to be logged in the SQL Server Log file and/or the Microsoft Windows NT/Microsoft Windows 2000 application log.

D. **Correct:** The message string can contain substitution variables similar to the C language printf function, as in the following example:

```
RAISERROR('The current database ID is:%d', 16, 1, @DBID)
```

70-229.04.01.002

► Correct Answers: B

A. **Incorrect:** If a stored procedure runs completely, the results of @@ERROR will not show an error, because the stored procedure ran, even though the results were not what you expected. This is much like a function in other coding languages, where the function itself runs to completion and does not return an error, but the code within the function might not complete the desired actions.

B. **Correct:** This is the best approach. Inside each inner stored procedure, check the validity of the logic, which should include @@ERROR to ensure that there were no errors. @@ROWCOUNT can also be used if the success of the stored procedure can be determined by the number of rows that were affected. A return code should then be returned to the outer stored procedure. The outer stored procedure should be executed with a variable already declared to trap the return code. The outer stored procedure can continue depending on the result of this variable.

C. **Incorrect:** There is no need to include a transaction in the outer stored procedure because the requirements indicate that no actions need to be rolled back on an error. The stored procedure should just return an error message and stop execution.

D. **Incorrect:** The results of @@ROWCOUNT might not indicate the successful completion of all of the business requirements in the inner stored procedures.

70-229.04.01.003

▶ Correct Answers: A, B, and C

A. **Correct:** ROLLBACK TRAN will roll back any implicit or explicit transaction to the beginning or to a named savepoint.

B. **Correct:** If you specify a high enough severity code with RAISERROR, the transaction will roll back.

C. **Correct:** Division by zero or another run-time error will cause the transaction to roll back.

D. **Incorrect:** PRINT sends a message back to the calling application but will not cause the transaction to abort.

70-229.04.01.004

▶ Correct Answers: D

A. **Incorrect:** You cannot use any functions that change the transaction state, such as COMMIT or ROLLBACK. You also cannot start a transaction in a function. Every scalar SQL Server type, and also tables, can be returned by a user-defined function.

B. **Incorrect:** The first part of the answer is correct. You cannot use any statement that would change the state of a transaction; however, you can return a table, not just scalar types.

C. **Incorrect:** You cannot use any functions that change the transaction state, such as COMMIT or ROLLBACK. You also cannot start a transaction in a function. Every scalar SQL Server type, and also tables, can be returned by a user-defined function.

D. **Correct:** You cannot use any functions that would change the transaction state, but you can return a table from a user-defined function.

70-229.04.01.005

▶ Correct Answers: D

A. **Incorrect:** You can use an INSTEAD OF trigger on any table or view in your database. The INSTEAD OF trigger will override the default behavior of the statement you have executed (whether an INSERT, UPDATE, or DELETE) and allow you to write custom operations.

B. **Incorrect:** You can use both INSTEAD OF and AFTER triggers on distributed views as well as tables.

C. **Incorrect:** Although you can use an INSTEAD OF trigger with a distributed view, there is no limit on the number of same type triggers you can implement on a distributed view.

D. **Correct:** You can use INSTEAD OF triggers on any table, view, or partitioned view without limitation on the type of the trigger.

70-229.04.01.006

▶ Correct Answers: B

A. **Incorrect:** @@IDENTITY will return the last generated identity value for any table in the current session. In some situations, depending on the code run in the trigger, another table might have an identity value inserted, and this value could be returned in this trigger.

B. **Correct:** This is the best solution because this function returns the last identity generated in the current session and the current scope, which in this case is the trigger. @@IDENTITY will return the last generated identity value for any table in the current session. In some situations, depending on the code run in the trigger, another table might have an identity value inserted, and this value could be returned in this trigger. The IDENT_CURRENT function will return the last generated identity for the table passed as a parameter. There is a possibility that another session could have inserted a row into the table in the time between the insertion of the row by the trigger and the running of the IDENT_CURRENT function.

C. **Incorrect:** The IDENT_CURRENT function will return the last generated identity for the table passed as a parameter. There is a possibility that another session could have inserted a row into the table in the time between the insertion of the row by the trigger and the running of the IDENT_CURRENT function, depending on the amount of code and usage in the trigger. @@IDENTITY will return the last generated identity value for any table in the current session. In some situations, depending on the code run in the trigger, another table might have an identity value inserted, and this value could be returned in this trigger.

70-229.04.01.007

▶ Correct Answers: A

A. **Correct:** An output variable can be used to return a data value to the calling code. This is a very common method for returning scalar values from a stored procedure. The calling code must be aware of and capable of handling output parameters. Because only one value is expected, using an output parameter is more elegant than using a SELECT statement to obtain the results. Because the calling code does not need to work through multiple rows in the result set, the calling code is simpler.

B. **Incorrect:** @@ROWS does not return the result rows, but returns the number of rows that are affected by the immediately preceding command.

C. **Incorrect:** A stored procedure can return only an integer value as a result code.

D. **Incorrect:** Although simply using a SELECT statement will provide a return result, it is not the best method. Although the SELECT statement returns a scalar value, using an output parameter allows the calling code to assume one value and code for that result. Using the SELECT statement requires that calling code to handle the possibility of multiple rows, and to manage the results as if there were multiples. This requires more overhead than the output parameter method.

70-229.04.01.008

▶ Correct Answers: A

A. **Correct:** This is the best solution because it can be used inline almost anywhere in a command. It can be referenced in a SELECT statement and is guaranteed to return only a scalar value, so there would never be a problem with a subquery returning more than one result and then causing an error. Because a BCP command can use a query or a view as well as a table, this function can be used by the BCP utility as well.

B. **Incorrect:** There is no way to pass a parameter to a view, so in order to get the view to compile, the EmployeeID was left out, which does not meet the requirement

C. **Incorrect:** Although you could create a stored procedure, it would not be the best option because a stored procedure cannot be invoked everywhere, such as in a query, which is necessary to meet the requirement.

70-229.04.01.009

▶ Correct Answers: D

A. **Incorrect:** This global variable will return the number of successful and attempted connections since the server was started.

B. **Incorrect:** @@NESTLEVEL will return the nesting level of the stored procedures, not the nesting level of transactions.

C. **Incorrect:** This returns the status of the last fetch from any cursor currently open in the connection.

D. **Correct:** This will return the number of open transactions in the connection. The BEGIN TRANSACTION statement will increment the @@TRANCOUNT global variable by one. COMMIT TRANSACTION will decrement this value. ROLLBACK TRANSACTION will set this variable to 0.

OBJECTIVE 4.2

Enforce procedural business logic by using stored procedures, transactions, triggers, user-defined functions, and views.

With SQL Server you can encapsulate frequently used operations in a single unit. These stored procedures can be included in other stored procedures to implement complex business logic. The included and parent stored procedures share the same transaction, and their operation is atomic.

SQL Server provides two primary mechanisms for enforcing business roles and logic: constraints and triggers. **Triggers** are special stored procedures invoked in response to an INSERT, UPDATE, or DELETE statement. Triggers can query other tables and include complex Transact-SQL statements. A trigger and the statement that fires it are handled in a single transaction. Triggers can perform more complex tasks than constraints can. Unlike constraints, triggers can reference other tables in the database. Triggers are also able to evaluate the state of the table before and after the data modification. Multiple triggers of the same type, such as INSERT, UPDATE, or DELETE, allow multiple actions to be performed in response to the same operation.

Transactions are the basic unit for modifying data in an atomic, consistent, isolated, and durable way. A transaction is a sequence of operations that is performed as a single unit of work. A transaction can be used to encapsulate a business process, including stored procedures, user-defined functions, triggers, and so on.

Objective 4.2 Questions

70-229.04.02.001

You want to create a trigger for a table so you can verify that one of the column values exists in another table and do some manipulation with the data. If the value is not found, you want to roll back the current transaction. Which statement is true?

A. You cannot access another table from a trigger, but you can abort a transaction.

B. You can access another table from a trigger, but you cannot abort a transaction, just like a user-defined function.

C. The requirements can be accomplished with a trigger. The trigger will work correctly.

D. You can neither access another table nor control the outcome of a transaction using a trigger.

70-229.04.02.002

You have the following Transact-SQL stored procedure code. Which line has an error? (Choose all that apply.)

```
CREATE PROCEDURE Test AS
BEGIN
  IF (@@ERROR > 0) THEN
    ROLLBACK TRAN
  ELSE BEGIN
    INSERT INTO Logs(Message) values('It Worked!')
  END
END
NOT FOR REPLICATION
```

A. `CREATE PROCEDURE Test AS`

B. `IF (@@ERROR > 0) THEN`

C. ROLLBACK TRAN must be in a BEGIN…END block.

D. NOT FOR REPLICATION

70-229.04.02.003

You want to write a stored procedure that will have a transaction inside. You want to ensure that the stored procedure will roll back only the actions within the procedure if it is called from code in which a transaction has already been declared, leaving the outer transaction intact. You do not know the setting for the XACT_ABORT option. Your stored procedure must run without errors when there is no outer transaction declared as well. What is the best approach to meet these requirements?

A. You do not need to do anything special to the stored procedure because if it is already in a transaction, only the stored procedure will be rolled back.

B. Use the BEGIN TRANSACTION… ROLLBACK TRANSACTION construct within the stored procedure.

C. At the beginning of the stored procedure, use the SAVE TRANSACTION construct with a transaction name and the ROLLBACK TRANSACTION construct with the same name.

D. If @@TRANCOUNT <> 0, use the SAVE TRANSACTION construct with a transaction name; otherwise, use the BEGIN TRANSACTION construct with a transaction name and the ROLLBACK TRANSACTION construct with the same name.

70-229.04.02.004

What are the internal or special (conceptual) temporary tables in a trigger, and what functions can you use to test for column states?

```
CREATE TRIGGER MyTrigger on MyTable for INSERT, UPDATE, DELETE
    AS ...
```

A. These special tables are INSERTED, UPDATED, and DELETED. Column state functions are INSERT(), UPDATE(), DELETE().

B. These special tables are INSERTED and DELETED. Column state functions are UPDATE() and COLUMNS_UPDATED().

C. These special tables are UPDATED and DELETED. Column state functions are UPDATE(), COLUMNS_UPDATED().

D. If no special tables are available within a trigger, you have to access the data tables directly.

70-229.04.02.005

You have created a table as follows:

```
CREATE TABLE Test1 (Id INT)
```

You created the following INSTEAD OF INSERT trigger on this table:

```
CREATE TRIGGER Test1_IO ON Test1
INSTEAD OF INSERT
AS
BEGIN
  INSERT INTO Test1 SELECT ID+1 FROM INSERTED
END
```

You executed the following code:

```
INSERT INTO Test1 VALUES(1)
SELECT * FROM Test1
```

What will be the result?

A. Execution will fail because inside the trigger you are inserting into the same table, and the trigger gets called over and over again until it overflows the buffer.

B. The result will be 1 because the trigger would do an infinite loop and SQL Server will not execute it.

C. The code will execute successfully, and the result will be 2.

70-229.04.02.006

You need to work procedurally through a result set of rows from a table called Employee with a primary key of EmployeeID, returning the first name concatenated to the last name. You do not want to use a cursor because of the possible locking problems. Which of the following code snippets would best satisfy this requirement?

A.
```
DECLARE @ NextID INT
SELECT @ NextID = MIN( ID ) FROM Employee
WHILE @ NextID IS NOT NULL
BEGIN
  SELECT ID, FirstName + ' ' + LastName FROM Employee
    WHERE ID = @ NextID
  SELECT @ NextID = MIN( ID ) FROM Employee WHERE ID > @ NextID
END
```

B.
```
DECLARE @NextID INT
SELECT @ NextID = MIN( ID ) FROM Employee
BEGIN
  SELECT ID, FirstName + ' ' + LastName FROM Employee
    WHERE ID = @ NextID
  SELECT @ NextID = MIN( ID ) FROM Employee WHERE ID > @ NextID
END
```

C.
```
DECLARE @ NextID INT
SELECT @ NextID = MIN( ID ) FROM Employee
IF @ NextID IS NULL GOTO Finish
BEGIN
  SELECT ID, FirstName + ' ' + LastName FROM Employee
    WHERE ID = @ NextID
  SELECT @ NextID = MIN( ID ) FROM Employee WHERE ID > @nextid
END
Finish:
```

D.
```
DECLARE @ NextID INT
SELECT @ NextID = MIN( ID ) FROM Employee
WHILE @ NextID IS NOT NULL
BEGIN
  SELECT ID, FirstName + ' ' + LastName FROM Employee
    WHERE ID = @ NextID
END
```

70-229.04.02.007

You need to create a report that will output all of the Employee rows and the Orders they have in the Northwind database. You want to see a row for every Employee, but report only the order amounts if the Employee is in the WA region and the order date is greater than 07/12/1996. You need to output a row for each Employee even if the Employee does not have an order later than that date or is not in the WA region. Which of the following queries would produce the correct result?

A.
```
SELECT E.LastName, O.OrderID, O.OrderDate
FROM Employees E LEFT OUTER JOIN Orders O
ON E.EmployeeID = O.EmployeeID
AND O.OrderDate > '1996-07-12'
WHERE E.Region = 'WA'
ORDER BY E.LastName
```

B.
```
SELECT E.LastName, O.OrderID, O.OrderDate
FROM Employees E LEFT OUTER JOIN Orders O
ON E.EmployeeID = O.EmployeeID
WHERE E.Region = 'WA'
AND O.OrderDate > '1996-07-12'
ORDER BY E.LastName
```

C.
```
SELECT E.LastName, O.OrderID, O.OrderDate
FROM Employees E LEFT OUTER JOIN Orders O
ON E.EmployeeID = O.EmployeeID
AND E.Region = 'WA'
AND O.OrderDate > '1996-07-12'
ORDER BY E.LastName
```

D.
```
SELECT E.Lastname, O.OrderID, O.OrderDate
FROM Employees E LEFT OUTER JOIN Orders O
ON E.EmployeeID = O.EmployeeID
AND E.Region = 'WA' WHERE O.OrderDate > '1996-07-12'
ORDER BY E.LastName
```

Objective 4.2 Answers

70-229.04.02.001

▶ Correct Answers: C

A. **Incorrect:** You can both access another table from a trigger and control the outcome of the transaction.

B. **Incorrect:** You can access another table from a trigger. Although user-defined functions cannot control the outcome of a transaction, triggers can.

C. **Correct:** You can access tables from the trigger and control the outcome of the transaction.

D. **Incorrect:** Triggers, just like stored procedures, can do all kinds of access and transaction controls. Triggers are invoked by SQL Server, whereas stored procedures are called on behalf of the user.

70-229.04.02.002

▶ Correct Answers: B and D

A. **Incorrect:** This syntax is correct. You can also optionally define input parameters and return values when you define the stored procedure. You can define default values so that not all parameters must be passed each time when the stored procedure is being called.

B. **Correct:** The IF statement does not use THEN. THEN is used in many programming languages such as Microsoft Visual Basic or VBScript. The correct syntax is IF (condition).

C. **Incorrect:** If the IF condition precedes a single statement, you do not have to use BEGIN...END. On the other hand, if the IF condition precedes more than one statement, you have to use the BEGIN...END to enclose the statement block.

D. **Correct:** Stored procedures are created with NOT FOR REPLICATION as default behavior. If you want the stored procedure to be replicated, you must use FOR REPLICATION. NOT FOR REPLICATION will generate an error.

70-229.04.02.003

► Correct Answers: D

A. **Incorrect:** If the stored procedure is executed within a transaction and an error occurs within the stored procedure, all of the actions might not be rolled back without explicitly indicating which logic should be rolled back.

B. **Incorrect:** If there is a ROLLBACK called inside the stored procedure, all of the work will be rolled back up to that point, including the work from the outside calling code that would already been executed before the stored procedure. This is not the behavior needed to meet the requirements.

C. **Incorrect:** Using the SAVE TRANSACTION construct with a name and then using that name with the ROLLBACK construct at the beginning of the stored procedure will cause only the work within the procedure itself to be rolled back if there is an error. This meets one of the requirements. However, the stored procedure will not run by itself outside a transaction because there is no transaction to save.

D. **Correct:** This is the best approach. Using the SAVE TRANSACTION construct with a name and then using that name with the ROLLBACK construct at the beginning of the stored procedure will cause only the work within the procedure itself to be rolled back if there is an error. This meets one of the requirements. However, the stored procedure will not run by itself outside a transaction because there is no transaction to save. It is best to check the value of @@TRANCOUNT to determine whether you are currently in a transaction, and then either create a savepoint with SAVE TRANSACTION if there is a transaction already started, or create a new one with BEGIN TRANSACTION. The same transaction name can be used for either option, so the ROLLBACK TRANSACTION would use this name and would be valid whether the SAVE TRANSACTION or BEGIN TRANSACTION construct was used.

70-229.04.02.004

► Correct Answers: B

A. **Incorrect:** SQL Server does not have INSERT(), UPDATE(), or DELETE() functions.

B. **Correct:** The INSERTED table contains all newly inserted records and all updates on existing records, and DELETED holds all deleted records. You can check whether a column is being changed with the UPDATE() function. Also, you can use the COLUMNS _UPDATED_() function to get a bit pattern representation of the changed columns.

C. **Incorrect:** There is no UPDATED table. The special tables created are the INSERTED and DELETED tables, and the UPDATE() function can be used to test whether a particular column has been updated.

D. **Incorrect:** To see the changes made by or requested with the INSERT, UPDATE, or DELETE statements, SQL Server has to provide you with the changes. SQL Server creates two special tables within the scope of a trigger. INSERTED has all the new inserts and updates, and DELETED holds all the deleted records.

70-229.04.02.005

▶ Correct Answers: C

A. **Incorrect:** If, in your trigger, you execute a statement against the same table that the trigger is activated on, the trigger will not be called again. SQL Server protects itself from this type of infinite loop.

B. **Incorrect:** The trigger will execute successfully, and the result will be 2. SQL Server will not call a trigger if the event comes from within a trigger.

C. **Correct:** The code example is correct. SQL Server will not execute a trigger if the code would fire the trigger on the same table.

70-229.04.02.006

▶ Correct Answers: A

A. **Correct:** This is one way to emulate a cursor with control-of-flow language if there is a primary key that can be used to move through the result set. The WHILE construct allows the code inside to loop until the condition is met.

B. **Incorrect:** Because there is no control-of-flow language other than a BEGIN and END, there is no loop to move through the results one row at a time. This code will execute only once. A better way would be to store either the minimum or the maximum primary key, and then move through the result set one row at a time with a WHILE clause, filtering for the current key as you go, and then getting the next key before moving on.

C. **Incorrect:** There is no loop here, only a check for a null; therefore, this code will execute only once. A better way would be to store either the minimum or the maximum primary key, and then move through the result set one row at a time with a WHILE clause, filtering for the current key as you go, and then getting the next key before moving on.

D. **Incorrect:** This code will loop an infinite number of times (or until the server crashes). There is a loop being called with the WHILE construct, but there is no change to the value being checked, so the loop will run forever. A better way would be to store either the minimum or the maximum primary key, and then move through the result set one row at a time with a WHILE clause, filtering for the current key as you go, and then getting the next key before moving on.

70-229.04.02.007

▶ Correct Answers: C

A. **Incorrect:** Although this query uses a left outer join, it will not return a row for employees who are not in the WA region. The result set is restricted after the join by the WHERE clause, which would restrict the rows for any employee not in the WA region.

B. **Incorrect:** Although this query uses a left outer join, it will not return a row for employees who are not in the WA region or who have orders with dates later than the orderdate. The result set is restricted after the join by the WHERE clause, which would restrict the rows for any employee not in the WA region and having orders that do not meet the criteria.

C. **Correct:** This query will return the correct results because the restrictions are placed on the JOIN clause. The OUTER JOIN then allows all rows in the employee table to be output, even if they are not in the WA region or they have no orders after the criteria date.

D. **Incorrect:** Although this query uses a LEFT OUTER JOIN, it will not return a row for employees not having orders later than the criteria date. The result set is restricted after the join by the WHERE clause.

OBJECTIVE 4.3

Troubleshoot and optimize programming objects.

A number of tools and methods are available to troubleshoot and optimize programming objects, such as stored procedures, triggers, user-defined functions, and views. These include coding statements, such as the PRINT statement and RAISERROR, to track and monitor the values of variables, as well as query and table hints to optimize the data access in a Transact-SQL statement.

One of the most valuable tools for troubleshooting stored procedures is the Transact-SQL Debugger. This tool is available in the SQL Query Analyzer and includes the most common debugging options, such as using watch expressions, stepping through code, and setting breakpoints in code.

Objective 4.3 Questions

70-229.04.03.001

You have a Web-based Online Transaction Processing (OLTP) orders application that has a few problematic SELECT queries that join six different tables and request the retrieved results in different orders. These queries are taking too long to return the results to the user. Which of the following would be the easiest and most effective way to get better performance from these few queries? (Choose all that apply.)

A. Use the OPTION (FAST n) query hint.

B. Use the ROBUST PLAN query hint.

C. Create indexed views for the queries.

D. Rewrite the statement as a view.

70-229.04.03.002

You need to troubleshoot a stored procedure, determining what the results of a particular local variable are during the execution of the store procedure. Which of the following can help to troubleshoot this procedure? (Choose all that apply.)

A. Use the SET statement to set the local variable to another value.

B. Use the PRINT statement inside the procedure to print out the local variable contents.

C. Use the RAISERROR statement.

D. Use the SQL Query Analyzer Transact-SQL Debugger.

70-229.04.03.003

You have a database application that uses dynamic SQL. The only changes to the query are the values that are used in the WHERE clause. You would like to ensure that the execution plan generated by the optimizer at compile time will be reused on subsequent executions. Which of the following approaches can help ensure cached execution plan reuse? (Choose all that apply.)

A. Rewrite the statement using the sp_executesql system stored procedure and fully qualified names.

B. Rewrite the statement as a stored procedure, using input parameters for the WHERE clause substitution.

C. Rewrite the statement using fully qualified object names.

D. Rewrite the statement as a view.

70-229.04.03.004

You have designed a database application that will be used by a large numbers of users, and you want to ensure that SELECT queries against the Products table do not block transactions that might be inserting data into other tables in the database. The Products table does not change except during a nightly batch job that will adjust the Products table. Which of the following SELECT statement locking hints can be used to minimize locking in this scenario?

A. HOLDLOCK

B. NOLOCK

C. PAGLOCK

D. TABLOCK

70-229.04.03.005

You are evaluating the performance of your database. Your organization allows access to the database only through stored procedures, but you notice that some of the stored procedures are recompiling. Which of the following situations can cause a stored procedure to recompile? (Choose all that apply.)

A. Changes to a large percentage of the data in the underlying objects

B. Interleaving of data manipulation language with data definition language in the stored procedure

C. Cursors created in the stored procedure that reference a temporary table in a SELECT statement

D. Statements that reference temporary tables that were created outside the stored procedure

Objective 4.3 Answers

70-229.04.03.001

► Correct Answers: A and C

A. **Correct:** Selecting this option will cause the query to be optimized for the first number of rows that is supplied in the hint. This returns the first group of information to users as fast as possible, allowing the time that the user looks at the first group to be used to retrieve the rest of the results. This is especially helpful if you supply the approximate number of rows to the query hint that fills the first page on the user interface.

B. **Incorrect:** This will force the optimizer to use a query execution plan that will be best for the maximum row size. This plan will be executed at the expense of performance, so this would not be a good option for this scenario.

C. **Correct:** Creating an indexed view by creating a view for the problematic queries and then adding a clustered unique index on these views will cause the creation of a table that is maintained by the server. There is a modification cost for the extra maintenance that needs to be performed by the server for these tables, but the performance gains can be great. A number of requirements must be met for an indexed view to be used. Only the Enterprise Edition of SQL Server supports indexed views, and there are a number of other prerequisites.

D. **Incorrect:** Writing statements as a view will not cause a query to perform faster or retrieve results faster.

70-229.04.03.002

► Correct Answers: B, C, and D

A. **Incorrect:** Using the SET statement will not provide debugging or troubleshooting information by itself. It is simply an assignment statement.

B. **Correct:** The PRINT statement can be used to output the value of a local variable. Using the PRINT statement at critical points in the procedure can help to troubleshoot the procedure. The PRINT statement can accept only character or Unicode values, so variables with other data types will need to be converted before they can be used with the PRINT statement.

C. **Correct:** Although RAISERROR is generally used to output error messages to clients, it can also be used to troubleshoot Transact-SQL by using the statement at critical points in the code, outputting the value of the local variable at those points in the execution of the code.

D. **Correct:** This is an excellent tool to debug a stored procedure. It can be used only within the SQL Query Analyzer, so it cannot be used during actual procedure execution from a client. However, it is very powerful and can show the value of local variables (through the watch functionality) throughout the execution of the code. It also supports stepping through code and setting breakpoints. The Transact-SQL Debugger should not be used on a production server.

70-229.04.03.003

► Correct Answers: A and B

A. **Correct:** Using the sp_executesql system stored procedure and passing the changed parameter values can help to ensure that a cached execution plan can be reused. The optimizer will give an internal name to the query and treat it as a pseudo-stored procedure, reusing the plan when possible if only the parameter values change. All object names must be fully qualified for the optimizer to reuse the plan.

B. **Correct:** Using a stored procedure will provide the best chance of an execution plan being reused. Fully qualified names are not required because the procedure name by itself will cause the optimizer to recognize the plan. However, using a stored procedure does not ensure that a cached execution plan is reused every time because there are conditions that will cause a stored procedure to recompile, such as the use of temp tables and cursors.

C. **Incorrect:** Although the optimizer might be able to reuse an execution plan if the Transact-SQL statement is very simple and fully qualified object names are used, this is very rare, and the use of fully qualified names will not in itself ensure that a cached execution plan will be reused.

D. **Incorrect:** Writing statements as a view does not ensure cached execution plan reuse, and not all dynamic statements can be rewritten as views.

70-229.04.03.004

► Correct Answers: B

A. **Incorrect:** The HOLDLOCK hint will force a lock to be held during the duration of the transaction and sets the isolation level to SERIALIZABLE. This would cause more locking on the table, and hence more blocking than no table hint at all.

B. **Correct:** Using the NOLOCK hint in this scenario would be the best approach. This hint will hold the minimal locks on the Products table, and because this table does not change during the transaction period of the day, it would not be a problem as far as uncommitted data being read by users. This will provide the best concurrency and ensure that minimal locking is held during the transaction.

C. **Incorrect:** This would force the optimizer to take a page lock instead of a table lock, but it would not provide the minimal locking in this scenario.

D. **Incorrect:** This will force the optimizer to lock the entire table, producing much more locking, hence blocking, than might have been caused without the hint.

70-229.04.03.005

► Correct Answers: A, B, C, and D

A. **Correct:** If a sufficient number of data modifications have been made to the underlying objects (such as large insertions or deletions), the stored procedure might be recompiled. This could be considered a good thing because the optimizer might select a different execution plan based on the data changes.

B. **Correct:** Using statements that create or drop objects interleaved with SELECT statements or other data manipulation statements can cause recompilation. This occurs because the objects might not exist during the first compile, so the optimizer is not able to create an execution plan. If objects, such as temporary tables and indexes, need to be created in a stored procedure, it is best to try to create them at the beginning, before they are referenced.

C. **Correct:** Creating a cursor with the DECLARE CURSOR statement that uses a temporary table in the SELECT clause of the cursor can cause a stored procedure to recompile.

D. **Correct:** A reference to a temporary table that was created outside the stored procedure can cause a recompile. It is best to create the required temporary table in the stored procedure, ensuring that the data definition statements, such as the CREATE TABLE statements, do not interleave with any data manipulation statements, such as SELECT statements.

OBJECTIVE DOMAIN 5

Tuning and Optimizing Data Access

The Tuning and Optimizing Data Access domain focuses on how to use the three main tools provided by Microsoft SQL Server 2000 to evaluate data access performance. The tools are:

- SQL Query Analyzer
- SQL Profiler
- Index Tuning Wizard

The SQL Query Analyzer is a tool that will run queries, return results, and display the **execution plan** in a graphical manner. It is the first tool used to determine whether a query is optimized for the current **data distribution** and indexes.

The Index Tuning Wizard can be run from the SQL Query Analyzer to suggest and create recommended indexes based on the queries and data in the database.

The SQL Profiler provides a great deal of information about the events on one or more servers. The SQL Profiler can help determine slow-running queries, poor execution plans, locking, **deadlocking**, and many other events that can affect performance.

Three main areas are critical to SQL Server data access performance:

- Optimal execution plans
- Cached execution plans
- Minimal locking

The SQL Query Analyzer can be used to ensure that the query has an optimal plan. This involves evaluating the graphical plan output by the Analyzer to ensure that data access is fast, that only data needed is acquired, and that indexes are being used. A short-running query will also ensure that any locks that might be required are short.

The Index Tuning Wizard can be used to determine whether the best indexes have been created for the data distribution, and it can be run against a query to ensure that the optimal plan has been selected.

You can use stored procedures or the **sp_executesql** system stored procedure for ad hoc queries to ensure that an execution plan is cached. The SQL Profiler can also be used to monitor recompiles. Because there is substantial overhead for continuously recompiling a query or stored procedure, you should make an effort to cache as many queries as possible. The SQL Profiler can also be used to determine queries that are long-running, and hence might be holding locks for too long and blocking other connections.

All of these tools can also be used to monitor and troubleshoot performance.

Tested Skills and Suggested Practices

The skills that you need to successfully master the Tuning and Optimizing Data Access domain on the *Designing and Implementing Databases with Microsoft SQL Server 2000 Enterprise Edition* exam include:

- **Analyzing a query execution plan.**
  - Practice 1: Back up the Northwind database. Drop all of the indexes on the tables, and create a query for all of the order details for every order for a certain state.
  - Practice 2: Evaluate the execution plan and determine where the major cost of the query lies. Look especially for table scans and large numbers of rows being passed to the next step in the tree.
  - Practice 3: Rewrite the query in another manner. For instance, if you used joins, use a subselect. Run both queries at the same time in the same SQL Query Analyzer window, and determine which query method performs the best, as indicated by the batch cost. Save the results in a file for later comparison.
- **Analyzing indexes with the Index Tuning Wizard.**
  - Practice 1: Highlight the queries that you created in the previous Practice 1 in the SQL Query Analyzer, and then run the Index Tuning Wizard for all of the tables in the Northwind database. Create any indexes the wizard suggests.
  - Practice 2: Rerun both the queries and evaluate the execution plan. Evaluate the differences between the execution plans generated before the index creation and the plans after the indexes have been created.

- **Capturing, analyzing, and replaying SQL Profiler traces.**
  - Practice 1: Create and run a SQL Profiler trace using the SQLProfiler-TSQL_Duration template. Run a number of different queries in the SQL Query Analyzer, and then evaluate them in SQL Profiler, determining which queries run the longest.
  - Practice 2: Create and run a new SQL Profiler trace using the SQLProfiler-TSQL template. Add the Execution Plan event class to this trace, and evaluate the same queries that were run in Practice 1 for execution plans. Try to determine from the execution plan why one query produces a longer duration than another query.
  - Practice 3: Create and run a new SQL Profiler trace with the SQLProfiler-TSQL_Replay template. Open a new SQL Query Analyzer instance and run a number of queries. Save the trace to a trace file. Using the SQL Profiler, replay the trace, stepping through the statements one at a time.

Further Reading

This section lists supplemental readings by objective. Study these sources thoroughly before taking exam 70-229.

Objective 5.1

Microsoft Corporation. *MCSE Training Kit: Microsoft SQL Server 2000 Database Design and Implementation.* Redmond, Washington: Microsoft Press, 2001. Read and complete the practices in Lesson 1, Chapter 14, "Maintaining and Optimizing SQL Server Database."

Microsoft SQL Server 2000 product documentation. To access Books Online (BOL), click the Start button, point to Programs, then Microsoft SQL Server, and then click Books Online. Click the Contents tab, double-click "Optimizing Database Performance," and review "Query Tuning." Also, click the Contents tab and double-click the "Using the SQL Server" topic. Then review "SQL Query Analyzer Help" under "User Interface Reference."

Objective 5.2

Microsoft Corporation. *MCSE Training Kit: Microsoft SQL Server 2000 Database Design and Implementation.* Redmond, Washington: Microsoft Press, 2001. Read and complete the practices in Lesson 1, Chapter 14, "Maintaining and Optimizing SQL Server Database."

Microsoft SQL Server 2000 product documentation. To access Books Online, click the Start button, point to Programs, then Microsoft SQL Server, and then click Books Online. Click the Contents tab, and double-click the "Administering SQL Server" topic. Then review "Evaluating Performance" under "Monitoring Server Performance and Activity."

Objective 5.3

Microsoft Corporation. *MCSE Training Kit: Microsoft SQL Server 2000 Database Design and Implementation.* Redmond, Washington: Microsoft Press, 2001. Read and complete the practices in Lessons 1 and 2, Chapter 11, "Implementing Indexes."

Microsoft SQL Server 2000 product documentation. To access Books Online, click the Start button, point to Programs, then Microsoft SQL Server, and then click Books Online. Click the Contents tab, and double-click the "Creating and Maintaining Databases" topic. Then review "Designing an Index" under "Indexes."

Objective 5.4

Microsoft Corporation. *MCSE Training Kit: Microsoft SQL Server 2000 Database Design and Implementation.* Redmond, Washington: Microsoft Press, 2001. Read and complete the practices in Lessons 1 and 2, Chapter 11, "Implementing Indexes."

Microsoft SQL Server 2000 product documentation. To access Books Online, click the Start button, point to Programs, then Microsoft SQL Server, and then click Books Online. Click the Contents tab, and double-click the "Creating and Maintaining Databases" topic. Select "Index Tuning Wizard" and review "Indexes" under the "Designing an Index" topic.

Objective 5.5

Microsoft Corporation. *MCSE Training Kit: Microsoft SQL Server 2000 Database Design and Implementation.* Redmond, Washington: Microsoft Press, 2001. Read and complete the practices in Lesson 1, Chapter 14, "Maintaining and Optimizing SQL Server Database."

Microsoft SQL Server 2000 product documentation. To access Books Online, click the Start button, point to Programs, then Microsoft SQL Server, and then click Books Online. Click the Contents tab, and review the "Administering SQL Server" topic. Then review "Evaluating Performance" under "Monitoring SQL Server Performance and Activity."

OBJECTIVE 5.1

Analyze the query execution plan.

The **SQL Query Analyzer** produces a graphical representation of the execution plan of a specific query or group of queries. Understanding and analyzing this plan is your best method to ensure that your application is fast, accurate, and scalable. This analysis should be done more than just once. You should do it when you create the query, against a test database of a size that will reflect your production database, and then at larger sizes to understand what will happen as more data is acquired.

There are many things to look for in the analysis of the plan. Even though an index has been used by the optimizer, creating another, more selective, index might provide better performance. Evaluate your query for unnecessary table scans, for sorts that can be eliminated with the creation of another index, and for bookmarks that indicate that the optimizer needs to go back to the clustered index or heap table to cover the query.

You can also use the analyzer to evaluate the difference between alternate approaches; the SQL Query Analyzer will indicate what percentage of the entire batch optimization cost is allocated to each part of the batch.

The SQL Query Analyzer can also produce a server trace, a client trace, and other statistics, and it can be used to execute queries directly against a database. There are also tools for browsing the database objects, and for debugging code directly in the analyzer.

Objective 5.1 Questions

70-229.05.01.001

You run a query in the SQL Query Analyzer with the Show Execution Plan option enabled, and the following execution plan is displayed. The Orders table has a unique clustered index on the OrderID primary key, and a nonclustered index on the CustomerID column. The Customers table has only a unique clustered index on the CustomerID primary key. Why has the optimizer selected to do a sort on the Orders?

Examine the execution plan below.

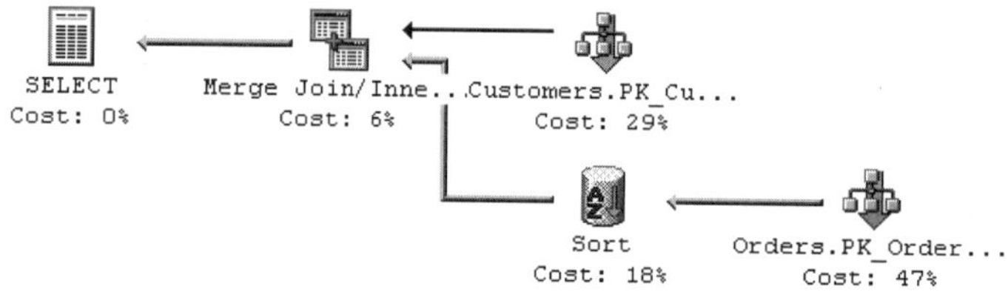

A. The optimizer has determined that a merge join would be the optimal method to retrieve this data. Because merge joins require both inputs to be in sorted order, it has added a sort operation to put the Orders table in CustomerID order, and it is using the CustomerID index on the Customers table, which will return the rows in CustomerID order as well.

B. Only merge joins can be used with clustered indexes.

C. Using an outer join will always force a merge join to be used.

D. Merge joins are the default join algorithms used by the SQL Server optimizer, unless you specify another type with a join hint in the query.

70-229.05.01.002

You run the following two queries in the same SQL Query Analyzer window with the Show Execution Plan option enabled. The following execution plan indicates that the first query's cost is 29.89 percent, relative to the batch cost of both queries. The Orders table has a unique clustered index on the OrderID primary key and a nonclustered index on the CustomerID column. The Customers table has only a unique clustered index on the CustomerID primary key. Why has the optimizer selected two different query plans when the joins are the same and there is no WHERE clause?

```
SELECT Customers.CompanyName, Orders.OrderID
FROM Customers LEFT OUTER JOIN Orders
ON Customers.CustomerID = Orders.CustomerID
SELECT *
FROM Customers LEFT OUTER JOIN Orders
ON Customers.CustomerID = Orders.CustomerID
```

Examine the execution plans below.

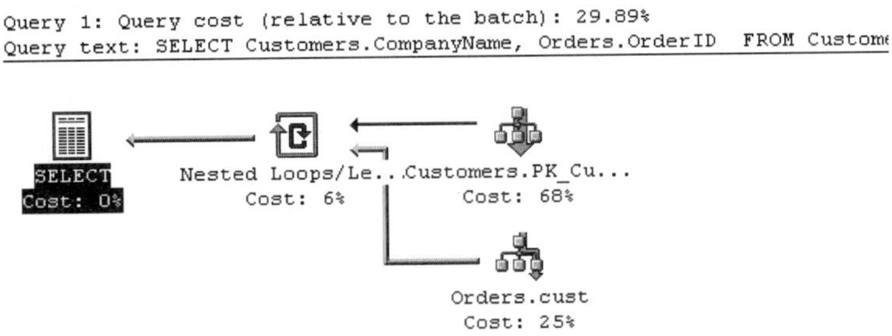

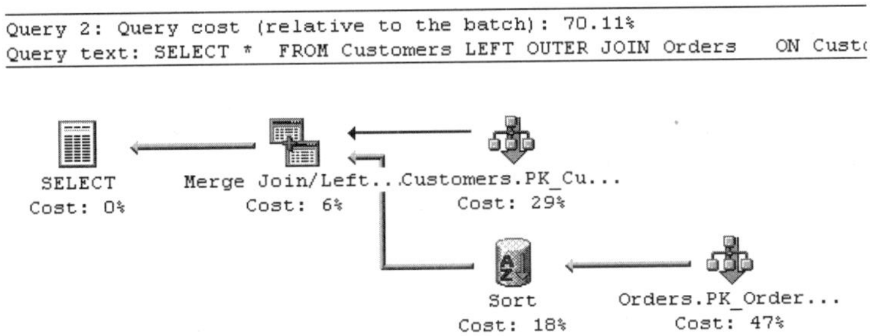

A. The optimizer has determined that a merge join would be the optimal method to retrieve this data. Because merge joins require both inputs to be in sorted order, it has added a sort operation to put the Orders table in CustomerID order, and it is using the CustomersID index on the Customers table, which will return the rows in CustomerID order as well.

B. Only merge joins can be used with clustered indexes.

C. Using an outer join will always force a merge join to be used.

D. Merge joins are the default join algorithms used by the SQL Server optimizer, unless you specify another type with a join hint in the query.

70-229.05.01.003

You run the following query in the Northwind database. On the Orders table there is a clustered index on the OrderID and a nonclustered index on the OrderDate columns. On the Customers table there is only a clustered index on the CustomerID. When the query is run, the following execution plan is displayed. (Please note that this assumes there is no index in the Northwind database on the OrderDate column.)

```
SELECT EmployeeID FROM Orders JOIN Customers
ON Orders.CustomerID = Customers.CustomerID
WHERE OrderDate > '01/15/1997'
```

Why is a bookmark being used in this plan?

Examine the execution plans below.

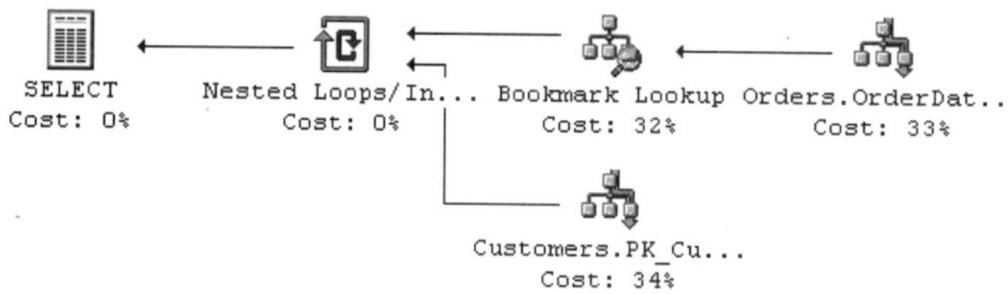

A. Because the EmployeeID is not included in the nonclustered index used to limit the results, the optimizer must use a bookmark to look up this value from the clustered index.

B. The nested loops join requires a sorted input, so the bookmark is used to look up the value of the EmployeeID from the clustered index.

C. The bookmark marks the place of each iteration through the nested loop.

70-229.05.01.004

You have noticed that some of the queries on a system are running longer than they used to. You know that statistics are important for ensuring that the optimizer can select the optimal index. How can you determine when the statistics were last updated for a particular index? (Choose all that apply.)

A. Use the SET STATISTICS IO command.

B. Run the DBCC SHOW_STATISTICS command for the index, and evaluate the UPDATE column for the last time the statistics were updated on the index.

C. Use the STATS_DATE system function to return the date an index was last updated.

D. Use the system stored procedure sp_statistics against the table.

Objective 5.1 Answers

70-229.05.01.001

► Correct Answers: A

A. **Correct:** The optimizer has selected a merge join, which requires the input from both sides to be in sorted order. It has selected to use the clustered index of each table because we have requested all the columns to be returned. Because there are no indexes other than the clustered index that contain all the column data, the optimizer considers it to be faster to retrieve all of the data from the clustered index on the Orders table, and then sort it in CustomerID order as an input to the merge join.

B. **Incorrect:** All of the three different join algorithms can be used with clustered indexes.

C. **Incorrect:** Although the optimizer in the join algorithm selection considers the join type, it does not require a merge join.

D. **Incorrect:** There is no default join algorithm for the optimizer that will always be used unless indicated otherwise.

70-229.05.01.002

► Correct Answers: A

A. **Correct:** The optimizer has selected a merge join, which requires the input from both sides to be in sorted order. It has selected to use the clustered index of each table because we have requested all of the columns to be returned. Because there are no indexes other than the clustered index that contain all of the column data, the optimizer considers it to be faster to retrieve all of the data from the clustered index on the Orders table, and then sort it in CustomerID order as an input to the merge join.

B. **Incorrect:** All of the three different join algorithms can be used with clustered indexes.

C. **Incorrect:** Although the optimizer in the join algorithm selection considers the join type, it does not require a merge join.

D. **Incorrect:** There is no default join algorithm for the optimizer that will always be used unless indicated otherwise.

70-229.05.01.003

► Correct Answers: A

A. **Correct:** The nonclustered index on OrderDate is being used to limit the rows to those that meet the criteria. Because the EmployeeID column is not included in the nonclustered index, the EmployeeID must be pulled from the clustered index. The optimizer uses a bookmark to look up this value in the clustered index.

B. **Incorrect:** A nested loops join does not require a sorted input, and the bookmark is not needed to support the nested loops join.

C. **Incorrect:** A nested loops join does iterate through one input to the join, but the bookmark is not used to mark the place in this iteration. It indicates that data has to be retrieved from the clustered index, because it is not available in the selected index used for the criteria limitation.

70-229.05.01.004

► Correct Answers: B and C

A. **Incorrect:** The SET STATISTICS IO command will show the physical and logical reads for a SQL statement. It will not show any information about index statistics.

B. **Correct:** The DBCC SHOW_STATISTICS command will display a great deal of information about the distribution statistics for a particular index, including the last date the statistics were updated.

C. **Correct:** The STATS_DATE system function will show the date an index was last updated.

D. **Incorrect:** The system stored procedure sp_statistics will display a list of all of the indexes and statistics for a table or indexed view, but will not display the date the statistics were last updated.

OBJECTIVE 5.2

Capture, analyze, and replay SQL Profiler traces.

The SQL Profiler captures a number of events and data about these events in a file that can be used to analyze or replay these events. This tool provides the best information on what is actually happening on the server. Trace information can be captured to files as well as to SQL tables, which allows queries to be run against the data for further analysis.

There are other methods of capturing data from the server as well. Trace flags can be set to capture information, such as deadlocks, and these can be output to an error log or a trace file. Customized traces can also be created to meet custom requirements. All of the data columns and events that are available in the SQL Profiler tool can be programmatically captured in a trace created in the SQL Query Analyzer. The trace option TRACE_PRODUCE_BLACKBOX is one of the trace options that can be set when creating a custom trace. This is the equivalent of the Flight Recorder that was available in SQL Server 7.0, and it will record the last 5 MB of trace information.

SQL Profiler traces can degrade server performance, so care should be taken to use the SQL Profiler appropriately.

Objective 5.2 Questions

70-229.05.02.001

SQL Profiler can perform many functions for monitoring SQL Server activity and performance. Which of the following functions can SQL Profiler perform? (Choose all that apply.)

A. Show a textual execution plan for queries that are run against a server.

B. Show a graphical execution plan for queries that are run against a server.

C. Capture when information is written to the transaction log.

D. Capture when the database and log files autogrow.

70-229.05.02.002

You need to determine whether a stored procedure is taking more than a second when it is run under load in your test environment. You want to be sure that a minimal amount of data is being captured in the SQL Profiler trace to ensure that performance is not being degraded. Which of the following SQL Profiler trace event classes and filters will provide you with the minimal information needed to determine whether this procedure ever runs longer than 1 second?

A. You run a trace with the SP:Completed and SQL:BatchCompleted event classes and keep the remaining default settings.

B. You run a trace with the SP:Starting event class, add a filter to capture only events with TextData such as the name of the stored procedure, and keep the remaining default settings.

C. You run a trace with the SP:Completed event class, add a filter to capture only events with TextData such as the name of the stored procedure, and remove all data columns allowed except the Duration data column.

D. You run a trace with the SP:Completed event class, add a filter to capture only events with TextData such as the name of the stored procedure, remove all data columns allowed except the Duration data column, and add a filter to capture only events with a duration greater than 1 second.

70-229.05.02.003

You would like to have a trace captured on a machine and then replay that trace on a test machine. Which of the following event classes will you need to capture to be able to replay the trace if no cursors are being used? (Choose all that apply.)

A. Audit Login

B. Audit Logout

C. Existing Connection

D. RPC:Starting

E. SQL:BatchStarting

70-229.05.02.004

You have been sent a trace that was created with enough information to replay in the SQL Profiler, and you need to analyze the trace for long-running events. Which of the following methods can best be used to see only the events with duration greater than 5 seconds, grouped by the SPID?

A. Open the trace and, on the Data Columns tab of the Trace Properties dialog box, add the duration data column to the Selected Data list, and add a filter for any duration greater than 5 seconds.

B. Open the trace and, on the Data Columns tab of the Trace Properties dialog box, add the SPID data column to the Selected Data list, and add a filter for any duration greater than 5 seconds.

C. Open the trace and, on the Data Columns tab of the Trace Properties dialog box, add the SPID and Duration data columns to the Selected Data list.

70-229.05.02.005

You have a reporting server that supports ad hoc queries against the database, and you need to determine the usage of one of the major tables. You would like to be able to find the number of times that the table is accessed within a day and keep this data in such a way that it can be analyzed later in Microsoft Excel or Microsoft Access. How might you best accomplish this?

A. Create a trace with the SQL:StmtStarting event class and the TextData data column included, and set a filter to capture only events in which the TextData data column contains the table name. Set the trace stop time for 24 hours later. When the trace is completed, save it to a trace table.

B. Create a trace with the SQL:BatchStarting and SP:Starting events and the TextData data column included. Set the trace stop time for 24 hours later.

C. Create a trace with the SQL:BatchStarting and SP:Starting class events and the TextData data column included and set a filter to capture only events in which the ObjectName contains the table name. Set the trace stop time for 24 hours later.

Objective 5.2 Answers

70-229.05.02.001

▶ Correct Answers: A, C, and D

A. **Correct:** By adding the Execution Plan event class from the Performance event category, a textual execution plan can be captured in the SQL Profiler trace.

B. **Incorrect:** The SQL Profiler cannot show a graphical execution plan, as in the SQL Query Analyzer.

C. **Correct:** Adding the TransactionLog event class from the Transactions event category will capture when data is written to the transaction log.

D. **Correct:** Adding the Data File Auto Grow and the Log File Auto Grow event classes from the Database event category will capture data about when these events occur.

70-229.05.02.002

▶ Correct Answers: D

A. **Incorrect:** The SP:Completed event class is needed for the stored procedure event capture, but the SQL:BatchCompleted class will capture T-SQL commands as well. Because no filter has been applied, all instances of the stored procedure would be captured, not just those with a duration greater than 1 second.

B. **Incorrect:** Although the SP:Starting event class will capture the stored procedure event, and the filter will allow only the stored procedure event you want, duration data is captured. The duration data can be captured only on completion of an event, not the start. You would also need to add a filter to capture only instances of the stored procedure execution that exceed 1 second.

C. **Incorrect:** This proposed solution will produce a very small trace, capturing only the duration, system process ID (SPID), and event class for the stored procedure. However, because there is no filter on duration, it will not limit the instances with execution times greater than 1 second.

D. **Correct:** This proposed solution will produce the smallest amount of data for this scenario, and it will capture only the events of the stored procedure that have a duration greater than 1 second. Because the trace is so small, you can be fairly sure that the profiling itself is not interfering with the server performance.

70-229.05.02.003

▶ Correct Answers: A, B, C, D, and E

A. **Correct:** The Audit Login event class will capture all of the connection data needed to connect the trace when it is replayed. This event is required.

B. **Correct:** The Audit Logout event class will capture all of the disconnection data needed to disconnect the trace when it is replayed, and it should be included to complete a trace completely.

C. **Correct:** The ExistingConnection event is needed to ensure that events are captured for events occurring on connections already open on the server once the trace capture is started.

D. **Correct:** The RPC:Starting event class is needed to capture stored procedures that are executed from a client using an RPC mechanism.

E. **Correct:** The SQL:BatchStarting event class will capture any Transact-SQL batch data needed to replay these events.

70-229.05.02.004

▶ Correct Answers: B

A. **Incorrect:** This will cause the data to be grouped by the duration column, not the SPID column, but it will filter out any event with duration greater than 5 seconds.

B. **Correct:** This proposed solution will group the data by SPID and filter out any events except those with a duration greater than 5 seconds. This will also make the trace file smaller and easier to manage and analyze.

C. **Incorrect:** This proposed solution will group the data by both SPID and Duration, not just by SPID, and all events, regardless of duration, will be included.

70-229.05.02.005

▶ Correct Answers: A

A. **Correct:** The SQL:StmtStarting event will be captured for all SQL Statements, not just the start of a batch. By filtering the TextData data column for occurrences that contain the table name, only the actual statements that include the table name will be captured. Saving the trace file to a SQL Server table allows it to be analyzed more easily because queries can be run against the table, and it can be accessed with Excel or Access.

B. **Incorrect:** The SQL:BatchStarting event with the TextData data column will give you every Transact SQL statement and stored procedure sent to the server and will not capture usage only of the main table. SQL:BatchStarting does not capture every SQL statement, only the start of a batch. It does not provide a good mechanism for analyzing in Excel or Access.

C. **Incorrect:** The ObjectName data column is not populated by the SQL:BatchStarting and SP:Starting events, so the filter will not be used, and all events will be captured. SQL:BatchStarting does not capture every SQL statement, only the start of a batch. This approach does not provide a good mechanism for analyzing in Excel or Access.

OBJECTIVE 5.3

Create and implement indexing strategies.

Optimal index design is critical for query performance in SQL Server. There are many things to consider when designing indexes, and care should be taken to re-evaluate indexes on a database as data and queries change.

Every table in a database can have one **clustered index** and as many **nonclustered indexes** as needed. Determining which columns should be indexed with a clustered index can be considered an art. In the Enterprise Edition of SQL Server, indexes can also be created on views, providing excellent performance for often-used, complex queries.

Considerations for creating and implementing indexes include:

- Clustered indexes
- Nonclustered indexes
- Covering indexes
- **Indexed views**
- Statistics

Objective 5.3 Questions

70-229.05.03.001

You are designing an indexing strategy for your database and are evaluating clustered index placement. Which of the following situations can be considered good candidates for a clustered index? (Choose all that apply.)

A. Columns that contain a small number of distinct values, such as Gender

B. Columns that are frequently changed

C. Primary keys

D. Queries that will return a large range of values, such as from a BETWEEN clause

70-229.05.03.002

You are designing an indexing strategy for your database and are evaluating nonclustered index placement. Which of the following situations can be considered good candidates for a nonclustered index? (Choose all that apply.)

A. Foreign keys

B. All of the columns that are commonly accessed by a query

C. A column with a few unique values

D. Queries that return a small number of results

70-229.05.03.003

You have a database system that has been running for quite some time, with a large amount of inserts. There are a number of nonclustered indexes and a clustered index on all of the main large tables. Over time, you see that inserts are slowing down. What could you do to enhance insert performance on the large tables?

A. Using SQL Enterprise Manager, set the fill factor option to a smaller number for all of the existing indexes.

B. Drop the existing indexes and rebuild them with a smaller fill factor.

C. Run DBCC INDEXDEFRAG.

Objective 5.3 Answers

70-229.05.03.001

▶ Correct Answers: C and D

A. **Incorrect:** Generally a clustered index is wasted on a column with a very small number of unique values because the optimizer might find it less expensive to do a table scan than use an index. A better choice is a column with a large number of distinct values.

B. **Incorrect:** Columns that are frequently changed are especially bad candidates for a clustered index because all nonclustered indexes use a clustered index key as their identifier, so changing the value of a clustering key requires any nonclustered indexes to be rebuilt. Also, the data must be kept in physical order in a clustered index, so changing data in a clustered column might require the entire row to be physically moved. There are obviously large performance penalties for this.

C. **Correct:** Because primary keys are often used in joins and often require fast single-row lookups in online transaction processing (OLTP) systems, a clustered index on a primary key can be advantageous, especially if the primary key is a small surrogate key. If there is no compelling reason to put a clustered index on another column, a good default strategy is to put the index on the primary key.

D. **Correct:** Queries that return a large range of values will be in physical order if there is a clustered index on that column, so this is a good candidate for a clustered index.

70-229.05.03.002

▶ Correct Answers: A, B, and D

A. **Correct:** A foreign key column is often used in a join, so this makes a good candidate for a nonclustered index. Because merge joins require sorted input, including a nonclustered index on foreign keys can help ensure that the optimizer can consider a merge join as a possible inexpensive option.

B. **Correct:** This is called a "covering index," and it will allow a query to access only the nonclustered index without having to read data from the clustered index, eliminating accessing both the index and the main data.

C. **Incorrect:** Columns with a few unique values are not good candidates for any index because it is generally cheaper for the optimizer to do a table scan than to use an index in this situation.

D. **Correct:** Queries that do not return a large number of results are good candidates for nonclustered indexes. Because there is a good possibility that the data page will need to be accessed as well in combination with the index when a nonclustered index is used, retrieving small result sets will not cause performance problems.

70-229.05.03.003

► Correct Answers: B

A. **Incorrect:** Although setting the fill factor to a smaller value would probably be a good strategy for a table with many inserts, only when an index is created is the new fill factor followed. Changing the fill factor on all of the existing indexes will not produce smaller numbers of page splits.

B. **Correct:** Changing a fill factor is useful only when an index is created, so dropping and re-creating indexes with a smaller fill factor will leave more space open on each page. A system with a large number of inserts will therefore cause fewer page splits with a smaller fill factor.

C. **Incorrect:** The DBCC INDEXDEFRAG command will defragment and compact data and index pages, taking into account the original fill factor of the indexes when they were created. However, it cannot be used to change the fill factor so that more space is available on data and index pages as inserts are performed.

OBJECTIVE 5.4

Improve index use by using the Index Tuning Wizard.

The Index Tuning Wizard can be used to suggest and create optimal indexes for a database. The wizard can be run against a workload or against a query inside the SQL Query Analyzer. It can be used to script suggested indexes for later implementation, or it can create the indexes immediately. The Index Tuning Wizard is quite flexible in the configuration settings offered, can be run for a fast, intermediate, or thorough analysis, and can include indexed views. It also can consume CPU time and cause performance degradation, so it should be used during non-peak-usage times. Also, any index changes to a system should be thoroughly tested before implemented.

The Index Tuning Wizard can perform the following functions:

- Identify the servers and database to tune
- Identify a workload to analyze
- Select tables to tune
- Analyze the data and make index recommendations
- Implement the index recommendations
- Recommend indexes to be dropped if they are not used

Objective 5.4 Questions

70-229.05.04.001

You have a database application that has been running for about six months, and there have been no changes to the indexes since their creation. What should you do to help ensure that the optimal indexes have been created, and that indexes that are not being used are dropped?

A. Create a trace in SQL Profiler to capture an appropriately sized workload and run the Index Tuning Wizard against this workload.

B. Drop all existing indexes and run the Index Tuning Wizard against each of the common queries in the SQL Query Analyzer.

C. Create a small test database with a small number of rows for each table. Run the Index Tuning Wizard against this test database, and then implement the recommendations on the production server.

D. Run the Index Tuning Wizard against an appropriate workload created in the SQL Profiler with the Keep All Existing Indexes check box selected.

70-229.05.04.002

Which of the following will the Index Tuning Wizard not make recommendation on? (Choose all that apply.)

A. Primary key constraints

B. System tables

C. Queries that refer to tables in another database

D. Unique indexes

70-229.05.04.003

The Index Tuning Wizard can help optimize index usage. Which of the following are features of the Index Tuning Wizard? (Choose all that apply.)

A. Analyze a trace that was previously created in SQL Profiler.

B. The UI offers an option to limit the number of queries that are optimized.

C. The UI offers an option to limit the amount of memory used by the wizard.

D. Generate a script to create the recommended indexes for future use.

70-229.05.04.004

Which of the following will not be included for analysis by the Index Tuning Wizard? (Choose all that apply.)

A. Query, table, and index hints

B. Queries with quoted identifiers

C. Queries on a SQL Server 6.5 system

Objective 5.4 Answers

70-229.05.04.001

▶ Correct Answers: A

A. **Correct:** The Index Tuning Wizard will recommend indexes to be created and indicate those that are not being used from a workload created in SQL Profiler. The larger the workload, the better chance that the analysis will be optimal.

B. **Incorrect:** Dropping all indexes is a drastic approach, and indexes should not be dropped without understanding the consequences for query performance. It would take a long time to run the Index Tuning Wizard against every individual query, and this does not provide the most accurate information because a single query run by itself does not provide an accurate picture of what else might be happening on the server at the same time.

C. **Incorrect:** The Index Tuning Wizard might not recommend an index if a table has too few rows, just as the optimizer might not use an index if there too few rows. This is not a good strategy because the test database will not provide an accurate picture of the database for the Index Tuning Wizard.

D. **Incorrect:** Although the workload will give the Index Tuning Wizard a good reference for recommending indexes to be created, it will not recommend any to be dropped if the Keep Existing Indexes check box is selected. Therefore, unnecessary work might be performed to keep unneeded indexes up to date.

70-229.05.04.002

▶ Correct Answers: A, B, C, and D

A. **Correct:** The Index Tuning Wizard will not make a recommendation on a primary key constraint. Generally, you should always have some kind of index on a primary key constraint because this is a column that will be used often for joins and will always benefit from some kind of index, whether clustered or nonclustered.

B. **Correct:** Indexes should not usually be generated against system tables by users, so the Index Tuning Wizard will not consider these in its analyses.

C. **Correct:** The Index Tuning Wizard recommendation scope is only within the current database, so recommendations will not be made for an index on a table in another database, even if it is used within a query being analyzed.

D. **Correct:** The Index Tuning Wizard will not include unique indexes in its analysis.

70-229.05.04.003

► Correct Answers: A, B, and D

A. **Correct:** A workload that was created by monitoring a server with SQL Profiler can be saved to a trace file and then put into the Index Tuning Wizard. Capturing a full workload that exercises all the queries in a system can provide excellent information for tuning a system's queries and indexes.

B. **Correct:** One of the advanced options in the Index Tuning Wizard is an option to limit the number of queries that the wizard will analyze.

C. **Incorrect:** There is no option to limit the amount of memory used by the Index Tuning Wizard.

D. **Correct:** One of the features of the Index Tuning Wizard is the option to either execute the recommendations immediately or save them to a script to be further analyzed. It is recommended to never automatically execute the Index Tuning Wizard on a production server.

70-229.05.04.004

► Correct Answers: B and C

A. **Incorrect:** Query, table, and index hints are evaluated, but they will always be included in the Index Tuning Wizard and can actually cause the wizard to choose suboptimal indexes. It is best to remove hints before running the wizard.

B. **Correct:** The Index Tuning Wizard will not evaluate queries with quoted identifiers set on.

C. **Correct:** The Index Tuning Wizard cannot evaluate SQL Server 6.5 queries.

O B J E C T I V E 5 . 5

Monitor and troubleshoot database activity by using SQL Profiler.

The SQL Profiler is an excellent tool for auditing a SQL Server database. Security events, scheduled jobs, login failures, transaction log writes, and database and log file growth are some of the many events that can be monitored for both performance and security reasons. Auditing can be customized as needed and can be extensive enough to conform to the C2 auditing standards.

Operations that can cause performance problems can also be monitored, such as memory changes, large sorts, deadlocks, logical reads, physical writes, and DBCCs run during peak performance hours.

User activity can also be monitored, including determining the host name, application name, and Microsoft Windows NT domain name of logged-on users. The time that activities occur as well as the duration can also be monitored. SQL Profiler can also monitor errors, including severity.

Objective 5.5 Questions

70-229.05.05.001

Your corporation has policies in place that do not allow any administrative work to take place during the daytime hours. You think that someone might be granting permissions on objects during the day. You would like to determine whether object permissions are being granted during the day, and if so, as much information about the user as possible. Which is the best method to accomplish this?

A. You create a SQL Profiler trace that includes the SQL:BatchStarting event class, and includes the NTUserName and LoginName data columns.

B. You create a SQL Profiler trace that includes all of the Security Audit event classes, and only the TextData, SPID, and EventClass data columns.

C. You create a SQL Profiler trace that includes the Audit Object GDR Event event class and includes the NTUserName, LoginName, and StartTime data columns.

70-229.05.05.002

You receive a report that an application starts performing poorly when a large number of users are connected. You suspect that there might be transactions that have been left open for too long, because either queries are taking too long to complete, or user interaction is being requested in the middle of a transaction. What methods can you use to determine whether blocking is occurring in the database or transactions are being held open too long? (Choose all that apply.)

A. Run the system stored procedure sp_who on the server every few seconds, and look in the BLK column of the result set for any incidence of a blocking SPID.

B. Run the DBCC OPENTRAN command every few seconds.

C. Run the SQL Profiler and capture the Lock:Deadlock event, grouping by SPID.

D. Run the SQL Profiler and capture the event classes in the Transaction event category and the command being run, and then group the events by the Duration data column.

70-229.05.05.003

You have a large database application that uses many stored procedures. Whenever the server is rebooted, the system will run a bit more slowly, because each of the stored procedures is compiled before the execution plan. The application then tends to run faster. However, a certain number of stored procedures never seem to run faster. What is the best approach to determine whether these stored procedures are reusing a cached execution plan?

A. Run a SQL Profiler trace to capture the SP:Completed event grouped by the Duration data column.

B. Run a SQL Profiler trace capturing the SP:CacheHit, SP:CacheMiss, and SP:ExecContextHit events.

C. Run the system stored procedure sp_recompile against all of the stored procedures.

70-229.05.05.004

You have an application that is occasionally returning error message 1205, indicating that a deadlock has occurred and that the process has been chosen as the deadlock victim. Which of the following troubleshooting methods can you use to determine what query might be producing the deadlock? (Choose all that apply.)

A. Add the 1204 trace flag to the startup options of the server to capture deadlock information and output it to the error log. Restart the server.

B. Run the DBCC TRACEON (1204) command to capture deadlock information (trace flag 1204).

C. Capture the Lock:Deadlock and Lock:Deadlock Chain events in SQL Profiler.

D. Run the sp_lock system stored procedure.

Objective 5.5 Answers

70-229.05.05.001

▶ Correct Answers: C

A. **Incorrect:** The SQL:BatchStarting event class will capture the start of all SQL batches, which is too much information. The NTUserName and LoginName data columns will indicate the user information, but will not provide the time of the permissions statements.

B. **Incorrect:** Capturing all of the Security Audit events will capture too much information, and there are no data columns for the user or the time of the event.

C. **Correct:** The Audit Object GDR Event event class will capture events that occur when a GRANT, DENY, or REVOKE permission is made against an object. The NTUserName and LoginName data columns will indicate who is performing the operation, and the StartTime data column will show the time of the start of the permission event.

70-229.05.05.002

▶ Correct Answers: A, B, and D

A. **Correct:** Although this is a very simple method, it is a quick way to determine whether a connection is blocking another connection for a long period of time. The SPID identified in the BLK column will indicate the offending connection, which can then be further examined.

B. **Correct:** The DBCC OPENTRAN command will return information about the oldest open transaction in the database. If DBCC OPENTRAN continuously returns the same transaction as being open, there is a good possibility that something is holding the transaction open too long and should be investigated.

C. **Incorrect:** Capturing a deadlock can be helpful for troubleshooting, but it won't provide enough information to find a long-running transaction or blocking, because it will capture events that are caused by a deadlock, a special kind of locking situation that might never occur in the database.

D. **Correct:** The Transaction events grouped by Duration will provide information on the longest-running transaction, and include the SPID. This can then be used to further investigate the offending queries.

70-229.05.05.003

► Correct Answers: B

A. **Incorrect:** The SP:Completed event grouped by the Duration data column will show the longest-running stored procedure, which would not be helpful for determining execution plan reuse.

B. **Correct:** Capturing the cache hit, cache miss, and execution context hit events can help determine whether a stored procedure is being found in the cache and whether the execution plan is therefore reused.

C. **Incorrect:** The sp_recompile system stored procedure will cause a stored procedure to be recompiled the next time it is executed. It will not provide any information about execution plan reuse or producer recompilation.

70-229.05.05.004

► Correct Answers: A, B, and C

A. **Correct:** The 1204 trace flag will capture deadlock information and output it to the SQL Server error log. Once the server is restarted, any deadlocks will be captured, and information determining the SPIDs involved, and other diagnostic information, will be output as well. You can then use this information to evaluate the troublesome code.

B. **Correct:** The 1204 trace flag will capture deadlock information. With this DBCC command, the server does not need to be restarted. The SQL error log can then be examined for deadlock output and the offending queries investigated and corrected.

C. **Correct:** The SQL Profiler can capture deadlock information when it occurs, and these traces can then be evaluated to determine which processes are involved, and what the query running at the time was doing.

D. **Incorrect:** The sp_lock system stored procedure provides a great deal of valuable information on locking that is occurring on the database, including the lock type and the resources locked. However, it will not provide troubleshooting information about deadlocks.

OBJECTIVE DOMAIN 6

Designing a Database Security Plan

Microsoft SQL Server 2000 supports one of two security modes: Windows Authentication Mode (Windows Authentication) or Mixed Mode (Windows Authentication and SQL Server Authentication).

Windows Authentication Mode allows users to connect using Microsoft Windows NT 4 or Windows 2000 user accounts.

Mixed Mode Authentication allows users to connect using Microsoft Windows NT 4 or Windows 2000 user accounts or using SQL Server built-in authentication. SQL Server Authentication is provided only for backward compatibility.

When a blank login name is used for a SQL Server connection, SQL Server uses Windows Authentication. Windows Authentication has certain benefits over SQL Authentication primarily because of its integration with the Windows NT 4 and Windows 2000 operating system.

A SQL Server security system has two parts: access validation and permissions. Access validation includes the two security modes of SQL Server: Windows Authentication Mode or Mixed Mode. Permissions include object access permissions, such as INSERT, UPDATE, and DELETE, and object manipulation permissions, such as CREATE, ALTER, and DROP. SQL Server 2000 also introduced application security and application roles. Application security can be used to restrict users to access data only through a specific application, for example, Microsoft Excel. **Application roles** allow the application to take over the responsibility of user authentication.

Tested Skills and Suggested Practices

The skills that you need to successfully master the Designing a Database Security Plan objective on the *Designing and Implementing Databases with Microsoft SQL Server 2000 Enterprise Edition* exam include:

- **Controlling object access with GRANT and REVOKE.**
  - Practice 1: Create different user IDs.
  - Practice 2: Manage and modify user IDs.
  - Practice 3: Grant permissions to view and review the effects.
- **Controlling data access by using stored procedures, triggers, and user-defined functions.**
  - Practice 1: Create a stored procedure, grant user rights on it, and look at the behavior when you try to access it with different user IDs.
  - Practice 2: Create triggers and control user access with the triggers.
- **Creating and managing application roles.**
  - Practice 1: Create an application role.
  - Practice 2: Modify the application role.

Further Reading

This section lists supplemental readings by objective. Study these sources thoroughly before taking exam 70-229.

Objective 6.1

Microsoft SQL Server 2000 product documentation. To access Books Online, click the Start button, point to Programs, then Microsoft SQL Server, and then click Books Online. Click the Contents tab and double-click the "Administering SQL Server" topic. Then review "Managing Permissions" under "Managing Security."

Microsoft Corporation. *MCSE Training Kit: Microsoft SQL Server 2000 Database Design and Implementation*. Redmond, Washington: Microsoft Press, 2001. Read and complete the practices in Lesson 3 in Chapter 2, "Using Transact-SQL on a SQL Server Database," Lessons 1, 2, and 3 in Chapter 8, "Implementing Stored Procedures," Lessons 1, 2, and 3 in Chapter 9, "Implementing Triggers," Lessons 1, 2, and 3 in Chapter 10, "Implementing Views," and Lessons 1, 2, and 3 in Chapter 13, "Managing SQL Server Security."

Objective 6.2

Microsoft SQL Server 2000 product documentation. To access Books Online, click the Start button, point to Programs, then Microsoft SQL Server, and then click Books Online. Click the Contents tab and double-click the "Administering SQL Server" topic. Then review "Managing Permissions" under "Managing Security."

Microsoft Corporation. *MCSE Training Kit: Microsoft SQL Server 2000 Database Design and Implementation*. Redmond, Washington: Microsoft Press, 2001. Read and complete the practices in Lessons 1, 2, and 3 in Chapter 13, "Managing SQL Server Security."

Objective 6.3

Microsoft SQL Server 2000 product documentation. To access Books Online, click the Start button, point to Programs, then Microsoft SQL Server, and then click Books Online. Click the Contents tab and double-click the "Administering SQL Server" topic. Then review "Advanced Security Topics" under "Managing Security."

Microsoft Corporation. *MCSE Training Kit: Microsoft SQL Server 2000 Database Design and Implementation*. Redmond, Washington: Microsoft Press, 2001. Read and complete the practices in Lessons 1, 2, and 3 in Chapter 13, "Managing SQL Server Security."

OBJECTIVE 6.1

Control data access by using stored procedures, triggers, user-defined functions, and views.

In SQL Server 2000, the user must have sufficient rights to access and manipulate any object within the database.

Working with data or executing stored procedures requires permission. Object permissions are SELECT, INSERT, UPDATE, DELETE, and EXECUTE.

Statement permissions are activities involved in creating a database or an item in a database. Statement permissions are BACKUP DATABASE, BACKUP LOG, CREATE DATABASE, CREATE DEFAULT, CREATE FUNCTION, CREATE PROCEDURE, CREATE RULE, CREATE TABLE, and CREATE VIEW.

Permissions are managed by granting, denying, and revoking them.

GRANT allows a user to perform activities or work with data in the current database. Users can perform only the activities for which they have GRANT permission.

DENY prevents a user from performing activities or working with data in the current database and prevents the user account from inheriting permissions from other group or role memberships.

REVOKE removes the granted or denied permission only at the level revoked (user, group, or role).

Objective 6.1 Questions

70-229.06.01.001

You have a table called TABLE1 in your database. You do not want the user to access the table directly, but the user needs to insert data into the table. What can you do to fulfill this requirement? (Choose all that apply.)

A. Create a view and grant the user INSERT permission on the view.

B. Create a stored procedure and grant the user EXECUTE permission.

C. Create a stored procedure and grant the user EXECUTE and INSERT permissions.

D. You cannot fulfill this requirement.

70-229.06.01.002

In your database, you have a table with pregenerated account numbers. You do not want your users to access this table directly, but they need to be able to retrieve and remove one or more available account numbers from the table when they need them. You do not want them to execute any INSERT and UPDATE statement directly. This business logic sometimes needs to be executed as a part of a JOIN operation. How would you accomplish this?

A. Create a stored procedure and return the new account numbers.

B. Create a user-defined function and return the new account numbers.

C. You cannot fulfill this requirement.

70-229.06.01.003

You have a table called TABLE1 in your database and you are not connected to the database as the system administrator through the sa account. Why can't you set permission on a trigger for TABLE1?

A. Only the sa account can set permission on a trigger.

B. Only the creator or owner can set permission on a trigger.

C. You cannot set permission on a trigger.

70-229.06.01.004

You have OrderDetails and Products tables. You need to present the two tables as a single table using a join. You want ACCOUNTANTS to have read-only permissions, but you do not want them to access the tables directly and execute any other SELECT statements.

A. Create a view and make it perform the join. Grant SELECT permissions to ACCOUNTANTS.

B. Create two views and let ACCOUNTANTS execute a SELECT statement.

C. You cannot fulfill this requirement.

Objective 6.1 Answers

70-229.06.01.001

► Correct Answers: A and B

A. **Correct:** If a user has been granted INSERT permission to a view, it gives the user the ability to access all underlying tables even if he or she does not have rights on that table.

B. **Correct:** A user with EXECUTE permission on a stored procedure can accomplish work on underlying objects even if that user does not have any permission on the objects.

C. **Incorrect:** Although creating a stored procedure and granting the user EXECUTE permission would fulfill the requirements, you cannot grant INSERT permission on a stored procedure.

D. **Incorrect:** This requirement is easily fulfilled either by creating a view and granting INSERT permission to the user or by creating a stored procedure with EXECUTE permission for the user.

70-229.06.01.002

► Correct Answers: B

A. **Incorrect:** Although you can implement the required business login in a stored procedure and return a result set of new account numbers, the result set cannot be used as part of a JOIN operation. To be part of a JOIN operation, you must create a user-defined function and return a table as a return value.

B. **Correct:** Only a user-defined function can fulfill the requirements. Although a stored procedure can do the business logic, it cannot return a result set in a form that can be used in a JOIN operation.

C. **Incorrect:** This requirement is easy to fulfill by creating a user-defined function. A user-defined function can implement the required business logic and return a table as a return value.

70-229.06.01.003

▶ Correct Answers: C

A. **Incorrect:** You cannot assign permission on a trigger. You must have the appropriate permissions on the table to do the required work. If you have the appropriate permissions, the trigger will work accordingly.

B. **Incorrect:** Triggers are part of a table and, because of that, you cannot set permission on a trigger. If you need to control access, you have to set permission on the table itself.

C. **Correct:** You cannot set permission on a trigger. If you need to set permission, you have to set it on the table or view.

70-229.06.01.004

▶ Correct Answers: A

A. **Correct:** The view can provide the join. ACCOUNTANTS do not need any permission on the tables, but they do need to have SELECT permission on the view. It will provide them with the required data, and it also prevents them from executing any query against these two tables.

B. **Incorrect:** Although ACCOUNTANTS would be able to execute the join, they would be also able to execute other queries against these two tables. You need to provide them only with the join of these tables and not allow them to execute anything else.

C. **Incorrect:** A view can provide the join. ACCOUNTANTS do not have to have any permission on the tables, but they do need to have SELECT permission on the view. It will provide them with the required data, and it also prevents them from executing any query against these two tables.

OBJECTIVE 6.2

Define object-level security including column-level permissions by using GRANT, REVOKE, and DENY.

In SQL Server, every user must have permission to access and manipulate data in the database. These permissions are granted, revoked, and denied by using the appropriate SQL Server Transact-SQL command: GRANT, REVOKE, and DENY.

The GRANT command allows a user to perform activities or work with data in the current database. Users can perform only the activities for which they have GRANT permission. These object-level security permissions are INSERT, UPDATE, DELETE, and EXECUTE.

DENY prevents a user from performing activities or working with data in the current database and prevents the user account from inheriting permissions from other group or role memberships.

REVOKE removes the granted or denied permission only at the level revoked (user, group, or role).

In SQL Server 2000, permissions can be granted on smaller entities such as objects. You can set permissions not only on objects, but also on the columns.

Objective 6.2 Questions

70-229.06.02.001

You need to grant the SYSOPER user permission to SELECT and INSERT on Table1. You also want SYSOPER to be able to grant SELECT permission to other users with SELECT permission only. Which code block is correct?

A.
```
GRANT SYSOPER on Table1 to SELECT,INSERT
GRANT SYSOPER on Table1 to GRANT SELECT
```

B.
```
GRANT SYSOPER on Table1 to SELECT, INSERT, GRANT SELECT
```

C.
```
GRANT SELECT, INSERT on Table1 to SYSOPER WITH GRANT SELECT
```

D.
```
GRANT SELECT on Table1 to SYSOPER WITH GRANT OPTION
GRANT INSERT on Table1 to SYSOPER
```

70-229.06.02.002

You granted SELECT permissions to the PUBLIC role. You granted the MANAGERS role the permission to INSERT, UPDATE, and DELETE. You created an ACCOUNTANTS role with INSERT and UPDATE permissions. If a user is part of both ACCOUNTANTS and MANAGERS, which database operations is the user allowed?

A. The user will be able to SELECT, INSERT, and UPDATE but not to DELETE.

B. The user will be able to perform only the first granted role's permitted operations.

C. The user will be able to perform all four actions: SELECT, INSERT, UPDATE, and DELETE.

D. If a user belongs to at least one permission role other than PUBLIC, the user will not inherit the permissions of PUBLIC. Users will be able to INSERT, DELETE, and UPDATE, but not to SELECT.

70-229.06.02.003

You created table Test4 as follows:

```
CREATE TABLE Test4 (ID1 INT, ID2 INT)
GRANT SELECT (ID1) ON Test4 TO TEST
GRANT INSERT, UPDATE, DELETE ON Test4 TO Test
```

What would be the outcome if user Test executes the following code?

```
INSERT INTO Test4 (1,1)
SELECT * FROM Test4
```

A. Both INSERT and SELECT will execute successfully.

B. The INSERT statement would succeed, and the SELECT statement would fail.

C. The INSERT statement would fail, and the SELECT statement would succeed.

70-229.06.02.004

You want to prevent a user from executing an INSERT, UPDATE, or DELETE statement on a table. You want to be certain that if the user's role assignments change to a role that allows these operations, the user will still not be able to accomplish them. Which Transact-SQL command—DENY, REVOKE, or both—could accomplish this?

A. Neither command can be used to fulfill the requirements.

B. Both DENY and REVOKE could fulfill the requirements.

C. Only REVOKE can fulfill the requirements.

D. Only DENY can fulfill the requirements.

70-229.06.02.005

You do not want the ACCOUNTANTS role to have SELECT, UPDATE, and DELETE permission on the Trace table. You want to be certain if a user belongs to another role that has the right to access the Trace table, the user will still be able to do so. Which statement would accomplish this?

A. `DENY ACCOUNTANTS ON Trace TO SELECT, UPDATE, DELETE`

B. `REVOKE SELECT, UPDATE, DELETE on Trace FROM ACCOUNTANTS`

C. `REVOKE ACCOUNTANTS ON Trace TO SELECT, UPDATE, DELETE`

D. `DENY SELECT, UPDATE, DELETE ON Trace TO ACCOUNTANTS`

Objective 6.2 Answers

70-229.06.02.001

▶ Correct Answers: D

A. **Incorrect:** The syntax in this example is incorrect. The parameters for GRANT are first, the kind of access you want to assign, and second, the SQL Server object and to whom you are granting the rights.

B. **Incorrect:** If you want to grant a user certain rights and also enable the user to assign rights to other users, you have to do it in two separate statements.

C. **Incorrect:** Using the WITH GRANT option, you cannot specify what kind of permission the user can grant to other users. To fulfill the requirements, you have to execute two separate statements.

D. **Correct:** You must use two statements to both give a user permission to use specific commands and then to limit the user's ability to grant permission to other users to only a subset of those commands.

70-229.06.02.002

▶ Correct Answers: C

A. **Incorrect:** This user will inherit all permissions from all roles. If you do not want a user to have a given permission, you should revoke or deny it.

B. **Incorrect:** In SQL Server, we do not have a role that supersedes all other roles. This user will inherit all permissions from all roles.

C. **Correct:** The user will inherit the permissions from all roles. These roles cover all the required functionality.

D. **Incorrect:** The user will belong to all roles. PUBLIC is just another database role in SQL Server, such as MANAGERS and ACCOUNTANTS.

70-229.06.02.003

▶ Correct Answers: B

A. **Incorrect:** Test has permission to INSERT, UPDATE, and DELETE from Test4 but has only the right to SELECT from column ID1. SELECT ID1 FROM Test4 would execute successfully.

B. **Correct:** The INSERT statement would complete successfully because you granted Test INSERT, UPDATE, and DELETE permission on the whole table; however, you granted Test permission to SELECT only from ID1.

C. **Incorrect:** The INSERT statement would complete successfully because you granted Test INSERT, UPDATE, and DELETE permission on the whole table; however, you granted Test permission to SELECT only from ID1. SELECT ID1 FROM Test4 would execute successfully.

70-229.06.02.004

► Correct Answers: D

A. **Incorrect:** You can fulfill the requirement with the Transact-SQL command DENY.

B. **Incorrect:** DENY could prevent the user from inheriting permission through a group or role. REVOKE could remove only the previously granted or denied permission but would not affect inherited permissions.

C. **Incorrect:** REVOKE removes the previously granted or denied permission from the current user; it does not prevent the user from inheriting permission through a group or role.

D. **Correct:** DENY creates a record in the security system in the current database and prevents the user from inheriting permission through a group or role.

70-229.06.02.005

► Correct Answers: B

A. **Incorrect:** DENY could prevent the ACCOUNTANTS from having SELECT, UPDATE, and DELETE permissions on Trace, but it would also disable them from accessing Trace even if other roles would allow them to do so. The syntax of the statement is also incorrect.

B. **Correct:** This statement would prevent access on the object level, but it would not change the behavior of the inherited permissions.

C. **Incorrect:** Although REVOKE is the right command to achieve the desired permissions, the syntax of the statement is incorrect.

D. **Incorrect:** Although the statement syntax is correct, the statement would pose a more strict access control than was required. DENY would prevent the ACCOUNTANTS from having SELECT, UPDATE, and DELETE permissions on Trace, but it would also disable them from accessing Trace even if other roles would allow them.

OBJECTIVE 6.3

Create and manage application roles.

An application role is a new functionality in SQL Server 2000. It provides a way to restrict access to a database through a specific application. When an application role is activated for a connection by the application, the connection loses all permissions applied for the connection, including login, user account, roles, and so on. The connection gains the permissions associated with the application role. Application roles are applicable only to the database in which they exist. If an application using an application role needs to access another database, it must do so through the guest account. If a user by default would not have permission to access a table but the application needs to access the table to execute properly, the user permission will be overridden by the application permissions and the user will be able to access the table.

Application roles allow the application, rather than SQL Server, to manage user authentication. However, SQL Server still needs to authenticate the application when it accesses the database, so the application must provide a password to authenticate itself.

If ad hoc access to the database is not required, Windows NT 4 users and Windows 2000 users and groups do not need to be granted any permissions because all permissions can be assigned by the applications they use to access the database.

There are several options for managing application role passwords without hard-coding them into applications. An encrypted key stored in the registry or somewhere else, for which only the application has the decryption code, can be used. The application reads the key, decrypts it, and uses the value to set the application role.

Objective 6.3 Questions

70-229.06.03.001

You want to switch the current connection to use an application role. How would you accomplish this?

A. In the connection string, you would use the `Application Role=True` flag. Set the user name equal to the application name and the password equal to the application password.

B. Execute the sp_setapprole stored procedure to activate the permissions for an application role.

C. Execute `Setapplicationmode True, "Application Name","Password"`

D. This option is available only if the client connects using OLE DB and uses the `Application Role=True` flag.

70-229.06.03.002

Which connection type supports application role permissions and password encryption?

A. Only OLE DB

B. Only ODBC

C. Only DBLib

D. OLE DB and ODBC

70-229.06.03.003

If a connection is switched to application role permissions, what happens to the user's permissions and application role's permissions?

A. They are fused, and the connection will have both the user's and application role's permissions.

B. The user's permissions will be discarded, and only the application role's permissions will be used.

C. If the user has higher permissions, the user's permissions will be used; otherwise, the application role's permissions will be used.

D. Only those permissions will be available that exist in both the user's permissions and the application's permissions.

70-229.06.03.004

You found out that the application role's password has been compromised. You want to change the application role's password. How would you do it?

A. You cannot do it by just changing the password. You have to drop the current application role and re-create it.

B. You have to execute sp_approlechangepassword to change the application role's password.

C. You have to execute sp_approlepassword to change the application role's password.

D. You have to create a new application role with the new password and copy the permissions over with sp_copyapprolepermissions.

70-229.06.03.005

Can a connection use more than one application role, and is the application role valid in another database in the same SQL Server instance?

A. Connections can use more than one application role but are valid only in the current database.

B. Connections can use only one application role and are valid only in the current database.

C. Connections can use more than one application role and are valid in all databases in the same instance of SQL Server 2000.

D. Connections can use more than one application role and are valid in all databases.

Objective 6.3 Answers

70-229.06.03.001

► Correct Answers: B

A. **Incorrect:** You cannot connect as an application role to the database. You have to connect to the database and then switch your connection to use an application role using the sp_setapprole stored procedure.

B. **Correct:** You can switch an existing connection to application role permissions using the sp_setapprole stored procedure.

C. **Incorrect:** Setapplicationmode is not a valid Transact-SQL stored procedure. You have to use sp_setapprole to switch to application role permissions.

D. **Incorrect:** OLE DB, ODBC, and DBLib support application mode, but DBLib does not support encrypted passwords. Switching to application role permissions is achieved using sp_setapprole instead of a flag in the connection string.

70-229.06.03.002

► Correct Answers: D

A. **Incorrect:** OLE DB supports password encryption, and ODBC does also.

B. **Incorrect:** ODBC supports password encryption, and OLE DB does also.

C. **Incorrect:** Although DBLib supports application role permissions, it does not support password encryption. Password encryption is supported only by OLE DB and ODBC.

D. **Correct:** Both OLE DB and ODBC support password encryption, whereas DBLib does not.

70-229.06.03.003

► Correct Answers: B

A. **Incorrect:** When switching to application role permission, all information associated with the user, including login, username, and permissions, will be discarded, and only the application role's permissions will be used.

B. **Correct:** The application role's permission will be used, and the user-related information will be ignored and discarded from the connection.

C. **Incorrect:** SQL Server does not differentiate between higher-level permissions. When application role permission is used, all information associated with the user, including login, username, and permissions, will be discarded and only the application role's permissions will be available.

D. **Incorrect:** SQL Server will not fuse the users and the application role's permissions. When application role permission is used, all information associated with the user, including login, username, and permissions, will be discarded, and only the application role's permissions will be available.

70-229.06.03.004

▶ Correct Answers: C

A. **Incorrect:** You do not have to drop the application role and re-create a new one. You need to use the sp_approlepassword Transact-SQL stored procedure to change the application role's password.

B. **Incorrect:** You can change the application role's password, but sp_approlechangepassword is not a valid Transact-SQL stored procedure. The correct stored procedure is sp_approlepassword.

C. **Correct:** The application role's password can be changed without dropping the application role and re-creating it.

D. **Incorrect:** Although you can create a new application role, you cannot copy an application role's permissions to another application role. sp_copyapprolepermissions is not a valid Transact-SQL stored procedure. You have to use the sp_approlepassword Transact-SQL stored procedure to change the password.

70-229.06.03.005

▶ Correct Answers: B

A. **Incorrect:** A single connection can use only one application role at a time, and it is valid only in the database it was created in. If you need to access other databases through the same connection, you have to use the guest account.

B. **Correct:** SQL Server allows only one application role per connection, and it is valid only in the current database the application role was created in.

C. **Incorrect:** The application role is valid only in the database it was created in, and the connection can use only one application role at a given time.

D. **Incorrect:** A single connection can use only one application role at a time, and the role is valid only in the database it was created in.

Glossary

Symbols

@@ERROR A global variable that holds the error number for the last Transact-SQL statement executed. A value of 0 indicates no error. @@ERROR is reset after each statement is executed, so its value needs to be checked immediately after each Transact-SQL statement. The value must be saved to a local variable if it is to be used later in the code.

@@ROWS A global variable that holds the number of rows returned by the last Transact-SQL statement. @@ROWS is reset after each statement is executed, so its value should be saved to a local variable if it is needed later in the code.

A

ACID For a unit of work to qualify as a transaction, it must exhibit four characteristics: atomicity, consistency, isolation, and durability. *See also* atomicity, consistency, isolation, and durability.

ActiveX Data Objects (ADO) An easy-to-use application programming interface (API) that wraps OLE DB for use in languages such as Visual Basic, Visual Basic for Applications, Active Server Pages, and Microsoft Internet Explorer Visual Basic Scripting.

ADO *See* ActiveX Data Objects (ADO)

aggregate function A function that performs a calculation on a column in a set of rows and returns a single value.

aggregate query A query (SQL statement) that summarizes information from multiple rows by including an aggregate function such as SUM or AVG.

aggregation A collection of objects that makes a whole. An aggregation can be a concrete or conceptual set of whole-part relationships among objects.

American National Standards Institute (ANSI) An organization of American industry and business groups that develops trade and communication standards for the United States. Through membership in the International Organization for Standardization (ISO) and the International Electrotechnical Commission (IEC), ANSI coordinates American standards with corresponding international standards.

Analysis server The server component of Analysis Services that is specifically designed to create and maintain multidimensional data structures and provide multidimensional data in response to client queries.

ANSI *See* American National Standards Institute (ANSI)

ANSI SQL *See* SQL-92

API *See* application programming interface (API)

application programming interface (API) A set of routines available in an application, such as ADO, for use by software programmers when designing an application interface.

application role A SQL Server role created to support the security needs of an application. Application roles allow security permissions to be grouped at a custom level. Application roles do not have members, as do Windows NT or SQL groups. The ability to run an application gives a user access to objects that have application role permissions. Because application roles bypass standard permissions, the user is allowed permissions only during the connection, and permissions on underlying objects are lost after the connection is lost. Application roles require a password and can be used with both Windows Authentication Mode and Mixed Mode Authentication. *See also* Windows Authentication Mode, Mixed Mode.

atomic Either all of the transaction data modifications are performed or none of them are performed.

atomicity A state where all data modifications are performed, or none are performed; an atomic unit of work. Atomicity is one of the required characteristics for a transaction.

attribute A unit of data about an entity in a logical model. An attribute describes the entity. Just as an entity in a logical model translates to a table in the physical implementation, an attribute translates to a column.

authentication The process of validating that the user attempting to connect to SQL Server is authorized to do so. Microsoft SQL Server 2000 supports two authentication modes, Windows Authentication Mode and Mixed Mode.

availability A measure of how often a system is running and available to users.

AVG A SQL function to calculate the average of an expression.

B

BCP *See* bulk copy program (BCP)

binding In SQL application programming interfaces (APIs), binding is associating a result set column or a parameter with a program variable so that data is moved automatically into or out of a program variable when a row is fetched or updated.

browse mode A function that lets you scan database rows and update their values one row at a time. Several browse mode functions return information that an application can use to examine the structure of a complicated ad hoc query.

bulk copy program (BCP) A command-prompt bulk copy utility that copies SQL Server data to or from an operating system file in a user-specified format.

BULK INSERT A SQL statement to bulk copy data to a SQL Server instance within a SQL statement. The BULK INSERT command can be used from within a Transact-SQL statement.

business logic *See* business rules

business rules The logical rules that are used to run a business. Business rules can be enforced in the COM objects that make up the middle tier of a Windows DNA system. They can also be enforced in a SQL Server database using triggers, stored procedures, and constraints.

C

cache aging The mechanism of caching that determines when a cache row is outdated and must be refreshed.

cached execution plan A query execution plan that has been inserted into the execution plan, cached, and is available for reuse on the next execution of the query. Cached execution plans are one of the major performance features of SQL Server and allow the optimization step of query execution, which can be time-consuming, to be avoided on subsequent query executions. Execution plans are aged out of cache when they have not been accessed for a certain amount of time and each time the server is rebooted.

candidate key A column or set of columns that have a unique value for each row in a table. Each candidate key value uniquely identifies a single row in the table. Tables can have multiple candidate keys. One candidate key in a table is specified by the database designer to be the primary key for the table, and any other candidate key is called an *alternate key*.

cardinality A ratio that describes the number of relationship instances (for example, one-to-many).

CHECK constraint A constraint that defines which data values are acceptable in a column. You can apply CHECK constraints to multiple columns, and you can apply multiple CHECK constraints to a single column. When a table is dropped, CHECK constraints are also dropped.

child A member in the next lower level in a hierarchy that is directly related to the current member. For example, in a Time dimension containing the levels Quarter, Month, and Day, January is a child of Qtr1. *See also* parent.

clause In English Query, a sequence of related words within a sentence having both a subject and a predicate and functioning as either an independent or a dependent unit. In Transact-SQL, a subunit of a SQL statement. A clause begins with a keyword.

clustered index An index in which the logical order of the key values determines the physical order of the corresponding rows in a table. A clustered index uses a B-tree to store the path to the data, with the actual row data at the leaf level. The clustering key used in the clustered index is carried over to all nonclustered indexes created on the same table as the bookmark to the data in the clustered index.

collation A set of rules that determines how data is compared, ordered, and presented. Character data is sorted using collation information, including locale, sort order, and case sensitivity.

column In a SQL table, the area in each row that stores the data value for some attribute of the object modeled by the table. For example, the Employees table in the Northwind sample database models the employees of the Northwind Traders company. The LastName column in each row of the Employees table stores the last name of the employee represented by that row, the same way a Last Name field in a window or form would contain a last name.

COM *See* Component Object Model (COM)

Component Object Model (COM) A Microsoft specification for developing component software. Several SQL Server and database application programming interfaces (APIs), such as SQL-DMO, OLE DB, and ADO, are based on COM. Some SQL Server components, such as Analysis Services and English Query, store objects as COM objects.

concatenate To combine two or more character strings or expressions into a single character string or expression, or to combine two or more binary strings or expressions into a single binary string or expression.

consistency At the end of a transaction, all of the data must be consistent, with data integrity intact. Consistency is one of the four characteristics required for a unit of work to be considered a transaction.

constant A group of symbols that represent a specific data value. The format of a constant depends on the data type of the value it represents. For example, 'abc' is a character string constant, '123' is an integer constant, 'December 16, 1999' is a datetime constant, and '0x02FA' is a binary constant.

constraint A property assigned to a table column that prevents certain types of invalid data values from being placed in the column. For example, a UNIQUE or PRIMARY KEY constraint prevents you from inserting a value that is a duplicate of an existing value; a CHECK constraint prevents you from inserting a value that does not match a search condition; and NOT NULL prevents you from inserting a NULL value.

COUNT An aggregate function to return the number of items in a group.

CUBE A GROUP BY operator that aggregates results into a multidimensional cube.

cursor An entity that maps over a result set and establishes a position on a single row within the result set. After the cursor is positioned on a row, operations can be performed on that row or on a block of rows starting at that position. The most common operation is to fetch (retrieve) the current row or block of rows.

D

database A collection of information, tables, and other objects organized and presented to serve a specific purpose, such as searching, sorting, and recombining data. Databases are stored in files.

data distribution The distribution of values within a column of data. Data distribution is used to help the SQL Server query optimizer determine the optimal query execution plan.

data file In bulk copy operations, the file that transfers data from the bulk copy out operation to the bulk copy in operation. In SQL Server 2000 databases, data files hold the data stored in the database. Every SQL Server 2000 database has at least one primary data file and can optionally have multiple secondary data files to hold data that does not fit on the primary data file.

data integrity A state in which all the data values stored in the database are correct. If incorrect data values have been stored in a database, the database is said to have lost data integrity.

data mining model *See* mining model

data pump An OLE DB service provider that provides the infrastructure to import, export, and transform data between heterogeneous data stores using Data Transformation Services (DTS).

data source In ADO and OLE DB, the location of a source of data exposed to an OLE DB provider. *See also* ODBC data source.

The source of data for an object, such as a cube or dimension. It is also the specification of the information necessary to access source data. It sometimes refers to an object of ClassType clsDataSource.

data source name (DSN) The name assigned to an ODBC data source. Applications can use DSNs to request a connection to a system ODBC data source, which specifies the computer name and (optionally) the database to which the DSN maps.

Data Transformation Services (DTS) A set of objects and functions to assist with building data warehouses and data marts, as well as importing and exporting data between heterogeneous data sources.

data type An attribute that specifies what type of information can be stored in a column, parameter, or variable. System-supplied data types are provided by SQL Server; user-defined data types can also be created.

deadlock A situation in which two users, each having a lock on one piece of data, attempt to acquire a lock on the other's piece. Each user would wait indefinitely for the other to release the lock, unless one of the user processes is terminated. SQL Server detects deadlocks and terminates one user's process. Deadlocks can cause serious scalability problems.

default A data value, option setting, collation, or name assigned automatically by the system if a user does not specify the value, setting, collation, or name. An action taken automatically when certain events occur if a user has not specified the action to take.

DELETE A SQL statement that removes rows from one or more tables.

denormalize To introduce redundancy into a table in order to incorporate data from a related table. The related table can then be eliminated. Denormalization can improve efficiency and performance by reducing complexity in a data warehouse schema.

DENY A SQL statement that removes a permission from a user account and prevents the account from gaining permission through membership in groups or roles within the permission.

dimension A structural attribute of a cube, which is an organized hierarchy of categories (levels) that describe data in the fact table. These categories typically describe a similar set of members upon which the user wants to base an analysis. For example, a Geography dimension might include levels for Country, Region, State or Province, and City.

distributed query A single query that accesses data from multiple data sources.

distributed transaction A single transaction that accesses data from multiple data sources. Distributed transactions are managed by the Microsoft Distributed Transaction Coordinator (MS DTC) process and allow the four characteristics of transactions to be adhered to across disparate data sources.

domain In Windows 2000 security, a collection of computers grouped for viewing and administrative purposes that share a common security database. In relational databases, the set of valid values allowed in a column.

domain integrity An integrity mechanism that enforces the validity of entries for a given column. The mechanism, such as the CHECK constraint, can restrict the possible data values by data type, format, or range of values allowed.

DSN *See* data source name (DSN)

DTS *See* Data Transformation Services (DTS)

durability Ensures that once a transaction has completed, the results are permanent, even in the case of a system failure. Durability is one of the four characteristics required for a unit of work to be considered a transaction.

dynamic cursor A cursor that can reflect data modifications made to the underlying data while the cursor is open. Updates, deletes, and inserts made by users are reflected in the dynamic cursor.

E

encryption A method for keeping sensitive information confidential by changing data into an unreadable form.

entity integrity A state in which all the rows in a database have a not-null primary key value, all tables have primary keys, and no table has any duplicate primary key values. This ensures that there are no duplicate entries for anything represented in the database.

error log A text file that records system information from SQL Server.

execution plan The path and user context that the SQL Server query optimizer creates for the execution of a query. Every query must have an execution plan created by the SQL Server query optimizer, and plans can be cached for reuse, providing better performance.

explicit transaction A group of SQL statements enclosed within transaction delimiters. The first delimiter must be either BEGIN TRANSACTION or BEGIN DISTRIBUTED TRANSACTION, and the end delimiter must be one of the following: COMMIT TRANSACTION, COMMIT WORK, ROLLBACK TRANSACTION, ROLLBACK WORK, or SAVE TRANSACTION.

expression In SQL, a combination of symbols and operators that evaluate to a single data value. Simple expressions can be a constant, variable, column, or scalar function. Complex expressions are one or more simple expressions connected by operators.

extensibility The ability to be easily expanded or extended.

eXtensible Markup Language (XML) Self-describing data in a hypertext format. XML provides for hierarchical data display and is becoming the standard data format for the Internet. Along with the data, the column or attribute names are displayed, and a schema can be included as well.

F

fetch An operation that retrieves a row or block of rows from a cursor. Transact-SQL batches, stored procedures, and triggers use the FETCH statement to fetch from Transact-SQL cursors. Applications use application programming interface (API) fetch functions.

filegroup In SQL Server, a named collection of one or more files that forms a single unit of allocation or for administration of a database.

filter A set of criteria that controls the set of records returned as a result set. Filters can also define the sequence in which rows are returned.

filtering The ability to restrict data based upon criteria set in the WHERE clause of a SQL statement. For replication, filtering occurs on table articles defined in a publication. The result is partitions of data that can be published to Subscribers. *See also* partitioning.

FK *See* foreign key (FK)

float data type A data type that holds floating-point number data from –1.79E + 308 through 1.79E + 308. Float, double precision, and float(n) are SQL float data types.

foreign key (FK) The column or combination of columns whose values match the primary key (PK) or unique key in the same or another table.

function A piece of code that operates as a single logical unit. A function is called by name, accepts optional input parameters, and returns a status and optional output parameters. Many programming languages, including C, Visual Basic, and Transact-SQL, support functions. Transact-SQL supplies built-in functions, which cannot be modified, and supports user-defined functions, which can be created and modified by users.

G

global variable In SQL Server, a variable that can be referenced by multiple Data Transformation Services (DTS) tasks. In earlier versions of SQL Server, the term referred to the Transact-SQL system functions whose names start with two at signs (@@).

GRANT A SQL statement that applies permissions to a user account, which allows the account to perform an activity or work with data.

GROUP BY A clause added to a SQL statement to divide the data into groups.

GUID Globally unique identifier.

H

heterogeneous data Data stored in multiple formats. For example, data stored in a SQL Server database, a text file, and an Excel spreadsheet is heterogeneous data.

hierarchy A logical tree structure that organizes the members of a dimension such that each member has one parent member and zero or more child members.

I

IDENTITY A Transact-SQL function to insert a value automatically into a column when a new row is added. Identity columns allow for the starting number and the increment to be specified. Identity columns are commonly used for surrogate keys and are generally an integer value.

identity column A column in a table that has been assigned the identity property. The identity property generates unique numbers.

identity property A property that generates values that uniquely identify each row in a table. When inserting rows into a table that has an identity column, SQL Server generates the next identity value automatically based on the identity value last used and the increment value specified during column creation.

IEC *See* International Electrotechnical Commission (IEC)

implicit transaction A connection option in which each SQL statement executed by the connection is considered a separate transaction. Implicit transactions do not require the statements to be wrapped with a BEGIN…COMMIT TRAN clause.

index In a relational database, a database object that provides fast access to data in the rows of a table, based on key values. Indexes can also enforce uniqueness on the rows in a table. SQL Server supports clustered and nonclustered indexes. The primary key of a table is automatically indexed. In full-text search, a full-text index stores information about significant words and their location within a given column.

indexed view A SQL view where the data is stored in the database in the indexed order; an indexed view can provide performance gains.

INSERT A SQL statement that causes data to be entered as a row or rows into a table or view.

instance A copy of SQL Server running on a computer. A computer can run multiple instances of SQL Server 2000. A computer can run only one instance of SQL Server version 7.0 or earlier, although in some cases it can also be running multiple instances of SQL Server 2000.

int (integer) data type A SQL Server system data type that holds whole numbers from –2^31 (–2,147,483,648) through 2^31 – 1 (2,147,483,647).

integer In SQL Server 2000, a data type category that includes the ginint, int, smallint, and tinyint data types.

integrity constraint A property defined on a table that prevents data modifications that would create invalid data.

International Electrotechnical Commission (IEC) One of two international standards bodies responsible for developing international data communications standards. The IEC works closely with the International Organization for Standardization (ISO) to define standards of computing. They jointly published the ISO/IEC SQL-92 standard for SQL.

International Organization for Standardization (ISO) One of two international standards bodies responsible for developing international data communications standards. The International Organization for Standardization (ISO) works closely with the International Electrotechnical Commission (IEC) to define standards of computing. They jointly published the ISO/IEC SQL-92 standard for SQL.

ISO *See* International Organization for Standardization (ISO)

isolation Modifications made by one transaction are isolated from modifications made by another transaction. Isolation is one of the four characteristics required for a unit of work to be considered a transaction.

J

join As a verb, to combine the contents of two or more tables and produce a result set that incorporates rows and columns from each table. Tables are typically joined using data that they have in common. As a noun, the process or result of joining tables, as in the term *inner join* to indicate a particular method of joining tables. *See also* join column.

join column A column referenced in a join condition. *See also* join.

K

key A column or group of columns that uniquely identifies a row (PRIMARY KEY), defines the relationship between two tables (FOREIGN KEY), or is used to build an index.

key column A column referenced by a primary, foreign, or index key.

keyset cursor A cursor that shows the effects of updates made to its member rows by other users while the cursor is open but does not show the effects of inserts or deletes.

keyword A reserved word in SQL Server that performs a specific function, such as to define, manipulate, and access database objects.

L

linked cube A cube based on a cube defined on another Analysis server. *See also* publishing server, source cube, subscribing server.

linked server A definition of an OLE DB data source used by SQL Server 2000 distributed queries. The linked server definition specifies the OLE DB provider required to access the data and includes enough addressing information for the OLE DB provider to connect to the data. Any rowsets exposed by the OLE DB data source can then be referenced as tables, called *linked tables*, in SQL Server 2000 distributed queries.

lock A restriction on access to a resource in a multiuser environment. SQL Server locks users out of a specific row, column, or file automatically to maintain security or prevent concurrent data modification problems.

logical database design The design of a database based on business requirements, without regard for the physical implementation. Logical database design serves to verify the requirements, before physical implementation, which is much costlier to change, takes place.

logical data model A formal model of business data based on business requirements, without regard for the physical implementation. Generally, the logical model is the first tool designed for a database, and it serves to verify the business assumptions, before physical implementation of a database takes place.

M

macro A type of coding that is used like a function but actually consists of a set of instructions.

maintainability A measure of the ease of maintaining a system.

MAX A SQL function that returns the maximum value in an expression.

merge replication A type of replication that allows sites to make autonomous changes to replicated data and, at a later time, merge changes and resolve conflicts when necessary. *See also* snapshot replication, transactional replication.

metadata Information about the properties of data, such as the type of data in a column (numeric, text, and so on) or the length of a column. It can also be information about the structure of data or information that specifies the design of objects such as cubes or dimensions.

MIN A SQL function that returns the minimum value in an expression.

mining model An object that contains the definition of a data mining process and the results of the training activity. For example, a data mining model may specify the input, output, algorithm, and other properties of the process and hold the information gathered during the training activity, such as a decision tree.

Mixed Mode An authentication method that combines Windows Authentication and SQL Server Authentication. Mixed Mode allows users to connect to an instance of SQL Server, through either a Windows NT 4 or Windows 2000 user account or a SQL Server login.

N

nchar data type A fixed-length Unicode data type with a maximum of 4000 characters. Unicode characters use 2 bytes per character, and Unicode supports almost all international characters.

nonclustered index An index in which the logical order of the index is different from the physical, stored order of the rows on disk. The key used in a clustered index is also included in the nonclustered index as the bookmark to the physical data, which is stored in the clustered index. If there is no clustered index on a table, the nonclustered index will include a row identifier (RID) to bookmark the physical data.

normalization A set of database design rules that minimizes data redundancy and results in a database in which the database engine and application software can easily enforce integrity. There are a number of forms of normalization. Generally, online transaction processing systems are highly normalized and online analytical processing systems are highly denormalized.

ntext data type A variable-length Unicode data type that can hold a maximum of 2^30 – 1 (1,073,741,823) characters. ntext columns store a 16-byte pointer in the data row, and the data is stored separately.

nullability The attribute of a column, parameter, or variable that specifies whether it allows null data values.

nvarchar data type A variable-length Unicode data type with a maximum of 4000 characters. Unicode characters use 2 bytes per character, and Unicode supports almost all international characters. sysname is a system-supplied user-defined data type that is a synonym for nvarchar(128) and is used to reference database objects.

O

object In databases, one of the components of a database: a table, index, trigger, view, key, constraint, default, rule, user-defined data type, or stored procedure.

ODBC *See* Open Database Connectivity (ODBC)

ODBC data source The location of a set of data that can be accessed using an ODBC driver. Also, it is a stored definition that contains all of the connection information an ODBC application requires to connect to the data source. *See also* data source.

OLAP *See* online analytical processing (OLAP)

OLE DB A COM-based application programming interface (API) for accessing data. OLE DB supports accessing data stored in any format (databases, spreadsheets, text files, and so on) for which an OLE DB provider is available.

OLTP *See* online transaction processing (OLTP)

online analytical processing (OLAP) A technology that uses multidimensional structures to provide rapid access to data for analysis. The source data for OLAP is commonly stored in data warehouses in a relational database. Microsoft SQL Server 2000 supplies the Analysis Services, which are designed for OLAP applications.

online transaction processing (OLTP) A data processing system designed to record all of the business transactions of an organization as they occur. An OLTP system is characterized by many concurrent users actively adding and modifying data.

Open Database Connectivity (ODBC) A data access application programming interface (API) that supports access to any data source for which an ODBC driver is available. ODBC is aligned with the American National Standards Institute (ANSI) and International Organization for Standardization (ISO) standards for a database Call Level Interface (CLI).

OPENDATASOURCE A Transact-SQL function to allow ad hoc access to a remote server without using a linked server name.

OPENQUERY A Transact-SQL function to execute a passthrough query on a linked server.

OPENROWSET A Transact-SQL function to allow access to a remote server without using a linked server name, by providing all of the datasource information.

OPENXML A Transact-SQL function to open a rowset over an XML document, allowing the document to be part of a Transact-SQL query.

optimizer The SQL Server database engine component responsible for generating efficient execution plans for SQL statements.

ORDER BY A clause added to a SQL statement to determine the order of the returned result set.

outer join A join that includes all the rows from the joined tables that have met the search conditions, even rows from one table for which there is no matching row in the other join table. For result set rows returned when a row in one table is not matched by a row from the other table, a value of NULL is supplied for all result set columns that are resolved to the table that had the missing row.

P

parent A member in the next higher level in a hierarchy that is directly related to the current member. The parent value is usually a consolidation of the values of all of its children. For example, in a Time dimension containing the levels Quarter, Month, and Day, Qtr1 is the parent of January. *See also* child.

partition In Analysis Services, one of the storage containers for data and aggregations of a cube. Every cube contains one or more partitions. For a cube with multiple partitions, each partition can be stored separately in a different physical location. Each partition can be based on a different data source. Partitions are not visible to users; the cube appears to be a single object.

partitioning The process of replacing a table with multiple smaller tables. Each smaller table has the same format as the original table but contains a subset of the data. Each partitioned table has rows allocated to it based on some characteristic of the data, such as specific key ranges. The rules that define into which table the rows go must be unambiguous. For example, a table is partitioned into two tables. All rows with primary key values lower than a specified value are allocated to the other table. Partitioning can improve application processing speeds and reduce the potential for conflicts in multisite update replication. You can improve the usability of partitioned tables by creating a view. The view, created by a union of SELECT operations on all the partitioned tables, presents the data as if it all resided in a single table.

performance A measure of how fast a system can process requests. Performance is affected by many factors, including database and query design, physical disk systems, CPU capacity, and memory capacity. Performance is also measured in many different ways, depending on what kind of performance is requested, such as physical machine performance, throughput, or transactional rates.

physical database design A design for a database that is specific for the hardware and database program involved, usually an implementation derived from the logical database design.

PK *See* primary key (PK)

precision The maximum total number of decimal digits that can be stored, both to the left and right of the decimal point.

primary key (PK) A column or set of columns that uniquely identifies all the rows in a table. Primary keys do not allow null values. No two rows can have the same primary key value; therefore, a primary key value always uniquely identifies a single row. More than one key can uniquely identify rows in a table; each of these keys is called a *candidate key*. Only one candidate key can be chosen as the primary key of a table; all other candidate keys are known as alternate keys. Although tables are not required to have primary keys, it is good practice to define primary keys. In a normalized table, all of the data values in each row are fully dependent on the primary key. For example, in a normalized employee table that has EmployeeID as the primary key, all of the columns should contain data related to a specific employee. This table does not have the column DepartmentName because the name of the department is dependent on a department ID, not on an employee ID.

Publisher A server that makes data available for replication to other servers, detects changed data, and maintains information about all publications on the site.

publishing server An Analysis server that stores the source cube for one or more linked cubes. *See also* linked cube, subscribing server.

Q

Query Analyzer A tool provided with SQL Server that furnishes an environment in which to write and evaluate Transact-SQL statements. The Query Analyzer provides a graphical interface and tools for browsing the database objects, as well as help for functions.

R

RAID *See* redundant array of independent disks (RAID)

redundant array of independent disks (RAID) A method used with physical drives to provide fault tolerance. There are different levels of RAID that combine striping of data across the disks and mirroring of data in different configurations. Different RAID levels provide different mixes of cost, performance, and fault tolerance.

referential integrity A state in which all foreign key values in a database are valid. For a foreign key to be valid, it must contain either the value NULL or an existing key value from the primary or unique key columns referenced by the foreign key.

remote table A table stored in an OLE DB data source that is separate from the current instance of SQL Server. The table is accessed by either establishing a linked server definition or using an ad hoc connector name.

replication The process of copying and distributing data and database objects from one database to another and then synchronizing between databases for consistency.

result set The set of rows returned from a SELECT statement. The format of the rows in the result set is defined by the column list of the SELECT statement. An OLE DB result set is usually called a *rowset*.

REVOKE To remove a previously granted or denied permission from a user account role or group in the current database.

right outer join A type of outer join in which all rows in the rightmost table in the JOIN clause are included. When rows in the rightmost table are not matched in the table on the left, all result set columns that come from the left table are assigned a value of NULL.

role A SQL Server security account that is a collection of other security accounts that can be treated as a single unit when managing permissions. A role can contain SQL Server logins, other roles, and Windows logins or groups.

In Analysis Services, a role uses Windows security accounts to limit scope of access and permissions when users access databases, cubes, dimensions, and data mining models.

roll back To remove the updates performed by one or more partially completed transactions. Rollbacks are required to restore the integrity of a database after an application, database, or system failure.

ROLLUP A SQL operator used with the GROUP BY clause to aggregate a hierarchy of values.

rule A database object that is bound to columns or user-defined data types and specifies which data values are acceptable in a column. CHECK constraints provide the same functionality and are preferred because they are in the SQL-92 standard.

S

scalability A measure of the ability of a system to add more users or transactions.

scale The number of digits to the right of a decimal point in a number.

schema In the SQL-92 standard, a collection of database objects that are owned by a single user and form a single namespace. A namespace is a set of objects that cannot have duplicate names. For example, two tables can have the same name only if they are in separate schemas; no two tables in the same schema can have the same name. In Transact-SQL, much of the functionality associated with schemas is implemented by database user IDs. In database tools, schema also refers to the catalog information that describes the objects in a schema or database. In Analysis Services, a schema is a description of multidimensional objects such as cubes and dimensions.

script A collection of Transact-SQL statements used to perform an operation. Transact-SQL scripts are stored as files, usually with the .sql extension.

security A system to authenticate a user's identity and grant or deny access to different database objects. In SQL Server 2000, there are two types of authentication modes: Windows Authentication Mode and Mixed Mode. Security on objects can be granted on most objects, including columns within a table.

SELECT A Transact-SQL statement used to return data to an application or another Transact-SQL statement, or to populate a cursor. The SELECT statement returns a tabular result set consisting of data that is typically extracted from one or more tables. The result set contains only data from rows that match the search conditions specified in WHERE or HAVING clauses.

snapshot cursor *See* static cursor

snapshot replication A type of replication that distributes data exactly as it appears at a specific moment in time and does not monitor for modifications made to the data. *See also* merge replication, transactional replication.

source cube The cube on which a linked cube is based. *See also* linked cube.

sp_executesql A system stored procedure that allows a dynamic query statement to contain parameters and the execution plan to be reused. Using this procedure can produce performance enhancements when dynamic SQL code is required, and there is a good chance that the same code will be executed again.

SQL *See* Structured Query Language (SQL)

SQL database A database based on Structured Query Language (SQL).

SQL expression Any combination of operators, constants, literal values, functions, and names of tables and fields that evaluates to a single value. For example, use expressions to define calculated fields in queries.

SQL query A SQL statement, such as SELECT, INSERT, UPDATE, DELETE, or CREATE TABLE.

SQL Server authentication One of two mechanisms for validating attempts to connect to instances of SQL Server. Users must specify a SQL Server login ID and password when they connect. The SQL Server instance ensures that the login ID and password combination are valid before allowing the connection to succeed. Windows Authentication Mode is the preferred authentication mechanism.

SQL statement A SQL or Transact-SQL command, such as SELECT or DELETE, that performs some action on data.

SQL-92 The version of the SQL standard published in 1992. The international standard is ISO/IEC 9075:1992 Database Language SQL. The American National Standards Institute (ANSI) also published a corresponding standard (Data Language SQL X3.135-1192), so SQL-92 is sometimes referred to as *ANSI SQL* in the United States.

static cursor A cursor that shows the result set exactly as it was at the time the cursor was opened. Static cursors do not reflect updates, deletes, or inserts made to underlying data while the cursor is open. They are sometimes called *snapshot cursors*.

statistics Data that is stored and maintained by SQL Server to describe the selectivity and distribution of values in an index. Statistics must be kept up to date to ensure that the optimizer can select optimal query execution plans.

stored procedure A precompiled collection of Transact-SQL statements stored under a name and processed as a unit. SQL Server supplies stored procedures for managing SQL Server and displaying information about databases and users. SQL Server–supplied stored procedures are called *system stored procedures*.

Structured Query Language (SQL) A language used to insert, retrieve, modify, and delete data in a relational database. SQL also contains statements for defining and administering the objects in a database. SQL is the language supported by most relational databases and is the subject of standards published by the International Organization for Standardization (ISO) and the American National Standards Institute (ANSI). SQL Server 2000 uses a version of SQL called *Transact-SQL*.

subscribe To request data from a Publisher.

Subscriber A server that receives copies of published data.

subscribing server An Analysis server that stores a linked cube. *See also* publishing server, linked cube.

subscription An order that defines what data will be published, when, and to what Subscriber.

subscription database A database at the Subscriber that receives data and database objects published by a Publisher.

surrogate key An artificial attribute generated to perform as the key for a table, generally a small value.

system stored procedures A set of SQL Server-supplied stored procedures that can be used for actions such as retrieving information from the system catalog or performing administration tasks.

system tables Built-in tables that form the system catalog for SQL Server. System tables store all the metadata for an instance of SQL Server, including configuration information and definitions of all the databases and database objects in the instance. Users should not directly modify any system table.

T

table A two-dimensional object, consisting of rows and columns, used to store data in a relational database. Each table stores information about one of the types of objects modeled by the database. For example, an education database would have one table for teachers, a second for students, and a third for classes.

The columns of a table represent an attribute of the modeled object (for example, first name, last name, and address). Each row represents one occurrence of the modeled object. For example, one row in the Class table would record the information about an Algebra 1 class taught at 9:00 A.M., and another row would record the information about a World History class taught at 10:00 A.M.

timestamp data type A SQL Server system data type that consists of monatomically generated values that are always unique within a database.

TOP A SQL clause that will limit the results returned.

trace file A file used by SQL Profiler to record monitored events.

transaction A group of database operations combined into a logical unit of work that is either wholly committed or rolled back. A transaction is atomic, consistent, isolated, and durable (ACID).

transactional replication A type of replication in which an initial snapshot of data is applied at Subscribers, and then, when data modifications are made at the Publisher, the individual transactions are captured and propagated to Subscribers. *See also* merge replication, snapshot replication.

transaction log A database file in which all changes to the database are recorded. It is used by SQL Server during automatic recovery.

Transact-SQL The language containing the commands used to administer instances of SQL Server; to create and manage all objects in an instance of SQL Server; and to insert, retrieve, modify, and delete all data in SQL Server tables. Transact-SQL is an extension of the language defined in the SQL standards published by the International Organization for Standardization (ISO) and the American National Standards Institute (ANSI).

trigger A stored procedure that executes when data in a specified table is modified. Triggers are often created to enforce referential integrity or consistency among logically related data in different tables.

U

Unicode Unicode defines a set of letters, numbers, and symbols that SQL Server recognizes in the nchar, nvarchar, and ntext data types. It is related to but separate from character sets. Unicode has more than 65,000 possible values compared to a character set's 256, and Unicode requires twice as much storage space. Unicode supports characters for most written world languages.

Uniform Resource Locator (URL) A formatted string that references Internet resources.

UNIQUE constraint A constraint that enforces entity integrity on a nonprimary key. UNIQUE constraints ensure that no duplicate values are entered and that an index is created to enhance performance.

uniqueidentifier data type A data type containing a unique identification number stored as a 16-byte binary string used for storing a globally unique identifier (GUID).

unique index An index in which no two rows are permitted to have the same index value, thus prohibiting duplicate index or key values. The system checks for duplicate key values when the index is created and checks each time data is added with an INSERT or UPDATE statement.

update The act of modifying one or more data values in an existing row or rows, typically by using the UPDATE statement. Sometimes, the term update refers to any data modification, including insert, update, and delete operations.

UPDATE A SQL statement that changes the values in columns of one or more rows in a table.

URL *See* Uniform Resource Locator (URL)

user (account) A SQL Server security account or identifier that represents a specific user in a database. Each user's Windows account or SQL Server login is mapped to a user account in a database. Then, the appropriate permissions are granted to the user account. Each user account can only access data with which it has been granted permission to work.

user-defined data type A data type, based on a SQL Server data type, created by the user for custom data storage. Rules and defaults can be bound to user-defined data types (but not to system data types).

utility A SQL Server application run from a command prompt to perform common tasks.

V

view A database object that can be referenced the same way as a table in SQL statements. Views are defined using a SELECT statement and are analogous to an object that contains the result set of this statement.

W

WHERE clause The part of a SQL statement that specifies which records to retrieve.

Windows Authentication Mode One of the two mechanisms for validating attempts to connect to instances of SQL Server. Users are identified by their Windows user or group when they connect.

X

XML *See* eXtensible Markup Language (XML)

XPath A language used to query XML data where a schema is also attached.

Index

Symbols and Numbers

A

B

C

D

E

F

G

H

I

J

K

L

M

N

O

P

Q

R

S

T

U

V

W

X

Z

MICROSOFT LICENSE AGREEMENT

Book Companion CD

IMPORTANT—READ CAREFULLY: This Microsoft End-User License Agreement ("EULA") is a legal agreement between you (either an individual or an entity) and Microsoft Corporation for the Microsoft product identified above, which includes computer software and may include associated media, printed materials, and "on-line" or electronic documentation ("SOFTWARE PRODUCT"). Any component included within the SOFTWARE PRODUCT that is accompanied by a separate End-User License Agreement shall be governed by such agreement and not the terms set forth below. By installing, copying, or otherwise using the SOFTWARE PRODUCT, you agree to be bound by the terms of this EULA. If you do not agree to the terms of this EULA, you are not authorized to install, copy, or otherwise use the SOFTWARE PRODUCT; you may, however, return the SOFTWARE PRODUCT, along with all printed materials and other items that form a part of the Microsoft product that includes the SOFTWARE PRODUCT, to the place you obtained them for a full refund.

SOFTWARE PRODUCT LICENSE

The SOFTWARE PRODUCT is protected by United States copyright laws and international copyright treaties, as well as other intellectual property laws and treaties. The SOFTWARE PRODUCT is licensed, not sold.

1. **GRANT OF LICENSE.** This EULA grants you the following rights:
   - a. **Software Product.** You may install and use one copy of the SOFTWARE PRODUCT on a single computer. The primary user of the computer on which the SOFTWARE PRODUCT is installed may make a second copy for his or her exclusive use on a portable computer.
   - b. **Storage/Network Use.** You may also store or install a copy of the SOFTWARE PRODUCT on a storage device, such as a network server, used only to install or run the SOFTWARE PRODUCT on your other computers over an internal network; however, you must acquire and dedicate a license for each separate computer on which the SOFTWARE PRODUCT is installed or run from the storage device. A license for the SOFTWARE PRODUCT may not be shared or used concurrently on different computers.
   - c. **License Pak.** If you have acquired this EULA in a Microsoft License Pak, you may make the number of additional copies of the computer software portion of the SOFTWARE PRODUCT authorized on the printed copy of this EULA, and you may use each copy in the manner specified above. You are also entitled to make a corresponding number of secondary copies for portable computer use as specified above.
   - d. **Sample Code.** Solely with respect to portions, if any, of the SOFTWARE PRODUCT that are identified within the SOFTWARE PRODUCT as sample code (the "SAMPLE CODE"):
     - i. **Use and Modification.** Microsoft grants you the right to use and modify the source code version of the SAMPLE CODE, *provided* you comply with subsection (d)(iii) below. You may not distribute the SAMPLE CODE, or any modified version of the SAMPLE CODE, in source code form.
     - ii. **Redistributable Files.** Provided you comply with subsection (d)(iii) below, Microsoft grants you a nonexclusive, royalty-free right to reproduce and distribute the object code version of the SAMPLE CODE and of any modified SAMPLE CODE, other than SAMPLE CODE (or any modified version thereof) designated as not redistributable in the Readme file that forms a part of the SOFTWARE PRODUCT (the "Non-Redistributable Sample Code"). All SAMPLE CODE other than the Non-Redistributable Sample Code is collectively referred to as the "REDISTRIBUTABLES."
     - iii. **Redistribution Requirements.** If you redistribute the REDISTRIBUTABLES, you agree to: (i) distribute the REDISTRIBUTABLES in object code form only in conjunction with and as a part of your software application product; (ii) not use Microsoft's name, logo, or trademarks to market your software application product; (iii) include a valid copyright notice on your software application product; (iv) indemnify, hold harmless, and defend Microsoft from and against any claims or lawsuits, including attorney's fees, that arise or result from the use or distribution of your software application product; and (v) not permit further distribution of the REDISTRIBUTABLES by your end user. Contact Microsoft for the applicable royalties due and other licensing terms for all other uses and/or distribution of the REDISTRIBUTABLES.
2. **DESCRIPTION OF OTHER RIGHTS AND LIMITATIONS.**
   - **Limitations on Reverse Engineering, Decompilation, and Disassembly.** You may not reverse engineer, decompile, or disassemble the SOFTWARE PRODUCT, except and only to the extent that such activity is expressly permitted by applicable law notwithstanding this limitation.
   - **Separation of Components.** The SOFTWARE PRODUCT is licensed as a single product. Its component parts may not be separated for use on more than one computer.
   - **Rental.** You may not rent, lease, or lend the SOFTWARE PRODUCT.
   - **Support Services.** Microsoft may, but is not obligated to, provide you with support services related to the SOFTWARE PRODUCT ("Support Services"). Use of Support Services is governed by the Microsoft policies and programs described in the user manual, in "on-line" documentation, and/or in other Microsoft-provided materials. Any supplemental software code provided to you as part of the Support Services shall be considered part of the SOFTWARE PRODUCT and subject to the terms and conditions of this EULA. With respect to technical information you provide to Microsoft as part of the Support Services, Microsoft may use such information for its business purposes, including for product support and development. Microsoft will not utilize such technical information in a form that personally identifies you.
   - **Software Transfer.** You may permanently transfer all of your rights under this EULA, provided you retain no copies, you transfer all of the SOFTWARE PRODUCT (including all component parts, the media and printed materials, any upgrades, this EULA, and, if applicable, the Certificate of Authenticity), **and** the recipient agrees to the terms of this EULA.

- **Termination.** Without prejudice to any other rights, Microsoft may terminate this EULA if you fail to comply with the terms and conditions of this EULA. In such event, you must destroy all copies of the SOFTWARE PRODUCT and all of its component parts.

3. **COPYRIGHT.** All title and copyrights in and to the SOFTWARE PRODUCT (including but not limited to any images, photographs, animations, video, audio, music, text, SAMPLE CODE, REDISTRIBUTABLES, and "applets" incorporated into the SOFTWARE PRODUCT) and any copies of the SOFTWARE PRODUCT are owned by Microsoft or its suppliers. The SOFTWARE PRODUCT is protected by copyright laws and international treaty provisions. Therefore, you must treat the SOFTWARE PRODUCT like any other copyrighted material **except** that you may install the SOFTWARE PRODUCT on a single computer provided you keep the original solely for backup or archival purposes. You may not copy the printed materials accompanying the SOFTWARE PRODUCT.

4. **U.S. GOVERNMENT RESTRICTED RIGHTS.** The SOFTWARE PRODUCT and documentation are provided with RESTRICTED RIGHTS. Use, duplication, or disclosure by the Government is subject to restrictions as set forth in subparagraph (c)(1)(ii) of the Rights in Technical Data and Computer Software clause at DFARS 252.227-7013 or subparagraphs (c)(1) and (2) of the Commercial Computer Software—Restricted Rights at 48 CFR 52.227-19, as applicable. Manufacturer is Microsoft Corporation/One Microsoft Way/Redmond, WA 98052-6399.

5. **EXPORT RESTRICTIONS.** You agree that you will not export or re-export the SOFTWARE PRODUCT, any part thereof, or any process or service that is the direct product of the SOFTWARE PRODUCT (the foregoing collectively referred to as the "Restricted Components"), to any country, person, entity, or end user subject to U.S. export restrictions. You specifically agree not to export or re-export any of the Restricted Components (i) to any country to which the U.S. has embargoed or restricted the export of goods or services, which currently include, but are not necessarily limited to, Cuba, Iran, Iraq, Libya, North Korea, Sudan, and Syria, or to any national of any such country, wherever located, who intends to transmit or transport the Restricted Components back to such country; (ii) to any end user who you know or have reason to know will utilize the Restricted Components in the design, development, or production of nuclear, chemical, or biological weapons; or (iii) to any end user who has been prohibited from participating in U.S. export transactions by any federal agency of the U.S. government. You warrant and represent that neither the BXA nor any other U.S. federal agency has suspended, revoked, or denied your export privileges.

6. **NOTE ON JAVA SUPPORT.** THE SOFTWARE PRODUCT MAY CONTAIN SUPPORT FOR PROGRAMS WRITTEN IN JAVA. JAVA TECHNOLOGY IS NOT FAULT TOLERANT AND IS NOT DESIGNED, MANUFACTURED, OR INTENDED FOR USE OR RESALE AS ON-LINE CONTROL EQUIPMENT IN HAZARDOUS ENVIRONMENTS REQUIRING FAIL-SAFE PERFORMANCE, SUCH AS IN THE OPERATION OF NUCLEAR FACILITIES, AIRCRAFT NAVIGATION OR COMMUNICATION SYSTEMS, AIR TRAFFIC CONTROL, DIRECT LIFE SUPPORT MACHINES, OR WEAPONS SYSTEMS, IN WHICH THE FAILURE OF JAVA TECHNOLOGY COULD LEAD DIRECTLY TO DEATH, PERSONAL INJURY, OR SEVERE PHYSICAL OR ENVIRONMENTAL DAMAGE. SUN MICROSYSTEMS, INC. HAS CONTRACTUALLY OBLIGATED MICROSOFT TO MAKE THIS DISCLAIMER.

DISCLAIMER OF WARRANTY

NO WARRANTIES OR CONDITIONS. MICROSOFT EXPRESSLY DISCLAIMS ANY WARRANTY OR CONDITION FOR THE SOFTWARE PRODUCT. THE SOFTWARE PRODUCT AND ANY RELATED DOCUMENTATION ARE PROVIDED "AS IS" WITHOUT WARRANTY OR CONDITION OF ANY KIND, EITHER EXPRESS OR IMPLIED, INCLUDING, WITHOUT LIMITATION, THE IMPLIED WARRANTIES OF MERCHANTABILITY, FITNESS FOR A PARTICULAR PURPOSE, OR NONINFRINGEMENT. THE ENTIRE RISK ARISING OUT OF USE OR PERFORMANCE OF THE SOFTWARE PRODUCT REMAINS WITH YOU.

LIMITATION OF LIABILITY. TO THE MAXIMUM EXTENT PERMITTED BY APPLICABLE LAW, IN NO EVENT SHALL MICROSOFT OR ITS SUPPLIERS BE LIABLE FOR ANY SPECIAL, INCIDENTAL, INDIRECT, OR CONSEQUENTIAL DAMAGES WHATSOEVER (INCLUDING, WITHOUT LIMITATION, DAMAGES FOR LOSS OF BUSINESS PROFITS, BUSINESS INTERRUPTION, LOSS OF BUSINESS INFORMATION, OR ANY OTHER PECUNIARY LOSS) ARISING OUT OF THE USE OF OR INABILITY TO USE THE SOFTWARE PRODUCT OR THE PROVISION OF OR FAILURE TO PROVIDE SUPPORT SERVICES, EVEN IF MICROSOFT HAS BEEN ADVISED OF THE POSSIBILITY OF SUCH DAMAGES. IN ANY CASE, MICROSOFT'S ENTIRE LIABILITY UNDER ANY PROVISION OF THIS EULA SHALL BE LIMITED TO THE GREATER OF THE AMOUNT ACTUALLY PAID BY YOU FOR THE SOFTWARE PRODUCT OR US$5.00; PROVIDED, HOWEVER, IF YOU HAVE ENTERED INTO A MICROSOFT SUPPORT SERVICES AGREEMENT, MICROSOFT'S ENTIRE LIABILITY REGARDING SUPPORT SERVICES SHALL BE GOVERNED BY THE TERMS OF THAT AGREEMENT. BECAUSE SOME STATES AND JURISDICTIONS DO NOT ALLOW THE EXCLUSION OR LIMITATION OF LIABILITY, THE ABOVE LIMITATION MAY NOT APPLY TO YOU.

MISCELLANEOUS

This EULA is governed by the laws of the State of Washington USA, except and only to the extent that applicable law mandates governing law of a different jurisdiction.

Should you have any questions concerning this EULA, or if you desire to contact Microsoft for any reason, please contact the Microsoft subsidiary serving your country, or write: Microsoft Sales Information Center/One Microsoft Way/Redmond, WA 98052-6399.

PN 097-0002297

System Requirements

To use this book's Readiness Review compact disc, you need a computer equipped with the following minimum configuration:

- Microsoft Windows 95 or Microsoft Windows NT 4 with Service Pack 3 or later, or Microsoft Windows 98 or Microsoft Windows 2000 Professional
- Multimedia PC with a 75-MHz Pentium or higher processor
- 16 MB RAM for Windows 95 or Windows 98, or
- 32 MB RAM for Windows NT, or
- 64 MB RAM for Windows 2000
- Microsoft Internet Explorer 5.01 or later
- 17 MB of available hard drive space for installation (additional 70 MB minimum of hard disk space to install Internet Explorer 5.5 from the CD-ROM)
- A double-speed CD-ROM drive or better
- Super VGA display with at least 256 colors
- Microsoft Mouse or compatible pointing device

Proof of Purchase

0-7356-1251-X

Do not send this card with your registration.
Use this card as proof of purchase if participating in a promotion or rebate offer on *MCSE Microsoft® SQL Server™ 2000 Database Design and Implementation Readiness Review: Exam 70-229*. Card must be used in conjunction with other proof(s) of payment such as your dated sales receipt—see offer details.

MCSE Microsoft® SQL Server™ 2000 Database Design and Implementation Readiness Review: Exam 70-229

WHERE DID YOU PURCHASE THIS PRODUCT?

CUSTOMER NAME

Microsoft®

mspress.microsoft.com

Microsoft Press, PO Box 97017, Redmond, WA 98073-9830

OWNER REGISTRATION CARD

Register Today!

0-7356-1251-X

Return the bottom portion of this card to register today.

MCSE Microsoft® SQL Server™ 2000 Database Design and Implementation Readiness Review: Exam 70-229

FIRST NAME | MIDDLE INITIAL | LAST NAME

INSTITUTION OR COMPANY NAME

ADDRESS

CITY | STATE | ZIP

E-MAIL ADDRESS | ( ) PHONE NUMBER

U.S. and Canada addresses only. Fill in information above and mail postage-free.
Please mail only the bottom half of this page.